Safety Stock and Service Levels: A New Approach

**Shaun
Snapp**

Safety Stock: A New Approach

For information about this title or to order other books and/or electronic media, contact the publisher:

SCM Focus Press
PO Box 29502 #9059
Las Vegas, NV 89126-9502
http://www.scmfocus.com/scmfocuspress
(408) 657-0249

ISBN: 978-1-939731-52-4

Printed in the United States of America

Contents

CHAPTER 1: Introduction 1

CHAPTER 2: Safety Stock and Service Levels from a
             Conceptual Perspective 13

CHAPTER 3: The Common Ways of Setting Safety Stock 27

CHAPTER 4: Common Issues with Safety Stock Setting 39

CHAPTER 5: Common Issues with Service Level Setting 45

CHAPTER 6: Service Level Agreements 55

CHAPTER 7: Safety Stock and Service Levels in Inventory
             Optimization and Multi-Echelon Software 63

CHAPTER 8: A Simpler Approach to Comprehensively
             Setting Safety Stock and Service Levels 71

Conclusion 95

References 101

Author Profile 103

Abbreviations 106

Links Listed in the Book by Chapter 107

CHAPTER 1

Introduction

Safety stock is one of the best-known concepts in supply chain management. Every MRP application and every advanced planning application on the market has either a field for safety stock or can calculate safety stock. However, companies continue to struggle with the right level to set it.

Service levels are strongly related to safety stock, however companies also struggle with how to set service levels. The use of simplistic platitudes regarding the importance of maintaining high service levels is quite frequently used to disguise the fact that often those with the strongest opinions on the topic have little ability to quantify the appropriate service level for any particular item. That is they lack the ability to set differential service levels for a variety of items (much less an entire product location database). Just as importantly, they do not know how various service levels contribute to, or detract from, profitability.

A complicating factor is that many companies are influenced by Lean Principles (what is essentially recycled JIT, or *just in time* inventory), which proposes that there are always ways to further reduce inventory. Many companies – swept up by trends, and lacking a foundational understanding of forecasting or inventory management - confusingly declare the importance of both very high service levels AND the lowest inventory levels. Unfortunately, they do this in environments with high forecast inaccuracy.

On the topic of safety stock, it has been relatively easy for me to improve safety stock values when working in a number of companies, and this is for the following reasons:

1. *Distributed Responsibility:* Companies normally do not follow a solid method for setting safety stock – that is, the responsibility for setting safety stock is decentralized to those that do not have domain expertise in inventory management, and/or have a bias. This means that individuals with very narrow objectives are manually adjusting the safety stock.

2. *Poor Calculation Tools:* Companies are often unable to get some of the standard ways of calculating safety stock to work within their applications. Further, the tools available to companies within the majority of supply planning applications, while explained as "comprehensive" on the part of software vendors and many consulting companies,is actually very limited – for reasons that will be explained in great detail in this book.

Many individuals within companies complain to me that they are **unsure** at what level to set the safety stock. Safety stock is often covered from a simplistic

perspective with dynamic safety stock, which is based upon a very old formula and mistakenly considered as the "ultimate" state of safety stock because it auto-adjusts to changes in lead-time variability and forecast error.
Safety stock is often treated not as a value to be set with intelligence, but a valve to be adjusted to control the overall supply plan - something that safety stock is definitely not designed to be used for. Safety stock is a deceptively simple setting – seemingly so straightforward that one may question why I would devote half of a book to the subject (the other half being dedicated to service levels).

However, upon closer examination, I think you will agree that safety stock is much more complicated than it appears to be, and I do no mean simply how it is calculated. This underestimation of the implications of how safety stock is controlled is at the heart of why so many companies have difficulty mastering the topic.

In fact, even a full book on the topic would, I think, be warranted when one considers that so many companies have such problems in setting their safety stock values within an acceptable range. As a matter of fact, the guidance on safety stock available to companies is generally quite poor – bordering on appalling. The following list are reasons for this.

1. *Software Application Limitations:* There are far too many software vendors with low quality safety stock functionality.

2. *Software Consulting Limitations:* There are far too many consultants who recommend using the standard safety stock formulae without personally testing these formulae specifically or in a larger way in a production environment.

3. *Supply Chain Consultant Limitations:* There are also supply chain consultants that recommend following Lean Principles and arbitrarily reducing service levels – who also do not test the standard safety stock formula. Many of these consultants combine a misunderstanding of inventory management along with a misunderstanding of the safety stock functionality available within applications.

Up until several years ago, at the point where I intensively tested various safety stock techniques and developed a custom safety stock calculation approach,

I also thought that the standard formulas were far more effective at setting safety stock levels than I now know them to be. The reason for my change in view was extensively testing the standard safety stock formulas and finding them to come up short.

Secondly, except for when safety stock is calculated by a system which has both inventory optimization and multi-echelon capability, or calculated with the custom approach which I will describe in this book, the safety stock value that is calculated by all of the standard formulas is really too simple. Simplicity is not in itself a criticism, but it's really too simple to be used. And when a method of calculation is not useful, companies tend to migrate to managing their safety stock with less disciplined means.

You will be exposed in this book to the multiple ways of calculating safety stock. It's important to know the full story on safety stock, which means understanding both the simple and the complex methods. I also cover the maintenance issues that are common with safety stock. I critique the most common ways of determining safety stock, blending in my project experience.

I also cover how safety stock is set in a specialized type of supply planning system called inventory optimization and multi-echelon planning (MEIO). It is important to understand how MEIO safety stock works; however, most companies will never get to use a MEIO system, and MEIO systems come with some of their own limitations.

Therefore, I conclude the book by explaining a custom way of calculating safety stock that will greatly improve its calculation for many companies without having to implement an entirely new system like MEIO. As I personally developed this method, I believe it is the first time this has been explained in print.

This book also branches out into broader questions related to the important role that service level analysis and setting plays in the role of improving the profitability of a company. This intersects with research into how companies can intensively analyze which parts of the business are driving profits and which are not. Some results of this research are as follows:

"An enormous number of companies have large blocks of business that are unprofitable by any measure, and their managers agree that this is true. Yet few companies move aggressively to turn this around. Why is this so?

1. *Financial and management control information is not structured to surface the problem and opportunity areas. All departments have budgets. Sales has a revenue budget, and Operations has a cost budget. Yet, even if all departments make budget, the company can still be 30 to 40 percent unprofitable. Why? Because virtually all budgets start with a company's existing pattern of profitability (and embedded unprofitability).*

2. *Public companies have strong investor pressures that constrain managers from turning around embedded unprofitability. Many managers are concerned that eliminating unprofitable blocks of business would require reducing revenues substantially, and that this would hurt the company's stock price.[1]*

3. *In most companies, no one is responsible for systematically analyzing and improving profitability. Certainly, a CEO or general manager is responsible for profitability. But most of these individuals are focused on major strategic initiatives, important customer relationships and making sure their key managers make budget. The problem of analyzing the profitability of orders, accounts, products and services, and improving them through precisely targeted measures, falls through the cracks."*

— Islands of Profit in a Sea of Red Ink

---

[1] This is yet another example of the problem faced by companies that are public. However, this is one of the few times I can recall this specific issue being discussed. Therefore, Sales, Marketing, and the stock market value revenues over profit, and these are two very powerful forces shaping corporate strategy. They have a much more powerful effect on corporate strategy than Supply Chain. Therefore most companies are built to satisfy the interests or biases of the most influential interest.

This means that corporate strategy is not "logical" - it is simply responsive to whichever entity or entities are at the top of the food chain. This is also why so many private companies are run so much better than public companies. Private companies do not have the overwhelming pressure of the stock market to push corporate strategy to what fits within the mental box of what the stock market values.

This is a perfect example of where the detailed view supports the overall strategy. Dr. Jonathan Byrnes proposes that the best way to improve the profitability of a company is to analyze every single product/location combination and to reduce unprofitable and marginal items. This approach is consistent with the approach laid out in this book to setting safety stock and service levels for every product/location combination using an integrated calculator. Therefore, this book is not only focused on improving supply chain performance, but on improving the overall profitability of the company. The answer for improving profitability is a lot more obvious than many people realize.

Books and Other Publications on Safety Stock and Service Level

As with all my books, I performed a comprehensive literature review before I began writing. One of my favorite quotations about research is from the highly respected RAND Corporation, a "think tank" based in sunny Santa Monica, CA. They are located not far from where I grew up. On my lost surfing weekends during high school, I used to walk right by their offices with my friend — at that time having no idea of the institution's historical significance. RAND's *Standards for High Quality Research and Analysis* publication makes the following statement about how its research references other work.

> *"A high-quality study cannot be done in intellectual isolation:*
> *it necessarily builds on and contributes to a body of research*
> *and analysis. The relationships between a given study and*
> *its predecessors should be rich and explicit. The study team's*
> *understanding of past research should be evident in many aspects*
> *of its work, from the way in which the problem is formulated and*
> *approached to the discussion of the findings and their implications.*
> *The team should take particular care to explain the ways in which*
> *its study agrees, disagrees, or otherwise differs importantly from*
> *previous studies. Failure to demonstrate an understanding of*
> *previous research lowers the perceived quality of a study, despite any*
> *other good characteristics it may possess."*

There is no other book on safety stock. If you type 'safety stock' in to Amazon.com and include the term 'inventory,' (without the second part, you will end up with books on the stock market) all the books that come up at the top of the search results are related to inventory management. Safety stock is generally covered in these books in a theoretical sense. Typically, the reader will learn that safety stock is designed to manage both demand and supply variability, and then the book may include a few formulas for how to calculate safety stock.

One of my criticisms of much of the coverage of safety stock in books is that it presents these standard formulas as far more universal and far more effective than they actually are. Yes, they are the standard formulas, but that does not necessarily make them right for all circumstances - and in fact the formulas miss out on a lot of important, and I think better, techniques for calculating safety stock. This again is related to my observation that many people that write and consult on safety stock do not actually test the formulas that they are discussing, and in particular they do not test the formulas with real company data and then check to see if the safety stock which is calculated actually makes any sense to hold.

Therefore, this book will cover safety stock in a way that no other book has to date. While most of the other books that cover it in some capacity are quite deferential to the standard safety stock formula, this book provides an entirely different approach – one that is based upon intelligently setting the safety stock in a way that is consistent with other inventory management control values for the specific product/location combination as well as for other items.

The standard safety stock formulas offer quite limited functionality – and that the only safety stock calculation approach that is quite useful is contained within a category of supply planning applications that few companies will even implement. However, the approach outlined in the book is based upon real world experience of implementing safety stock in companies, and my experience of finding the standard formulae to be far less applicable than I was originally led to believe.

As far as service level is concerned, when I performed research into the books on service level management, there were a number of books on service level agreements, or SLAs. However, that is not the general study of service levels, but rather the study of how to setup and manage SLAs between companies. At this point in time, there is no book that focuses on service levels, although service levels are often covered in moderate detail in a variety of supply chain management books.

The topic of inventory optimization very much focuses on service levels because its objective function is to maximize service level while minimizing inventory. Therefore, service levels are covered in detail in my book *Inventory Optimization and Multi-echelon Planning Software*. There are also technical books on inventory optimization, but they are not generally useful for those that are not specialists in that area.

One interesting book on service levels is the book *Islands of Profit in a Sea of Red Ink*, which I quote in a number of places in this book. It is a strategic book, being something of a combined work on service level and profitability – issues that are a part of what is a long-running debate within companies; it is a debate which Supply Chain normally loses.

What has become standard in most companies is that the supply chain side of the business proposes more rational ways of setting service levels, while Sales and Marketing essentially march to the beat of a different drummer. They propose that only its objectives should drive the company and the job of the supply chain side of the business is to follow their lead. However, *Islands of Profit in a Sea of Red Ink* provides a powerful logic, as well as research, for why Sales, Marketing and Supply Chain should be equal partners in determining strategy.

This is something which is commonly stated as desirable, but is rarely actually in effect. This directly impacts service level, stocking level, the size of the SKU location database, and indeed the overall profitability of the company. It brings up the fact that the objective of the company is to maximize profits and not, as Sales and Marketing and even Wall Street propose, revenues. Once the framework of the argument can be switched to profits, this changes the criteria by which strategies are analyzed to become far more sustainable.

The Use of Screen Shots in the Book

I consult in some popular and well-known applications, and I've found that companies have often been given the wrong impression of an application's capabilities. As part of my consulting work, I am required to present the results of testing and research about various applications. The research may show that a well-known application is not able to perform some functionality well enough to be used by a company, and point to a lesser-known application where this functionality is easily performed. Because I am routinely in this situation, I am asked to provide evidence of the testing results within applications, and screen shots provide this necessary evidence.

Furthermore, sometime ago it became a habit for me to include extensive screen shots in most of my project documentation. A screen shot does not, of course, guarantee that a particular functionality works, but it is the best that can be done in a document format. Everything in this book exists in one application or another, and nothing described in this book is hypothetical.

Timing Field Definitions Identification

This book is filled with lists. Some of these lists are field definitions. The way to quickly identify which lists are field definitions is that they will be all in *italics*, while lists that are not field definitions will be only *italics* for the term defined, while the definition that follows is not in normal text.

How Writing Bias is Controlled at SCM Focus and SCM Focus Press

Bias is a serious problem in the enterprise software field. Large vendors receive uncritical coverage of their products, and large consulting companies recommend the large vendors that have the resources to hire and pay consultants rather than the vendors with the best software for the client's needs.

At SCM Focus, we have yet to financially benefit from a company's decision to buy an application showcased in print, either in a book or on the SCM Focus website. This may change in the future as SCM Focus grows – but we have been writing with a strong viewpoint for years without coming into any conflicts of interest. SCM Focus has the most stringent rules related to controlling bias and restricting commercial influence of any information provider. These "writing rules" are provided in the link below:

http://www.scmfocus.com/writing-rules/

If other information providers followed these rules, we would be able to learn about software without being required to perform our own research and testing for every topic.

Information about enterprise supply chain planning software can be found on the Internet, but this information is primarily promotional or written at such a high level that none of the important details or limitations of the application are exposed; this is true of books as well. When only one enterprise software application is covered in a book, one will find that the application works perfectly; the application operates as expected and there are no problems during the implementation to bring the application live.

This is all quite amazing and quite different from my experience of implementing enterprise software. However, it is very difficult to make a living by providing objective information about enterprise supply chain software, especially as it means being critical at some point. I once remarked to a friend that SCM Focus had very little competition in providing untarnished information on this software category, and he said, "Of course, there is no money in it."

The Approach to the Book

By writing this book, I wanted to help people get exactly the information they need without having to read a lengthy volume. The approach to the book is essentially the same as my previous books, and in writing this book I followed the same principles.

1. **Be direct and concise.** There is very little theory in this book and the math that I cover is simple. While the mathematics behind the optimization methods for supply and production planning is involved, there are plenty of books which cover this topic. This book is focused on software and, for most users and implementers of the software, the most important thing to understand is conceptually what the software is doing.

2. **Base on project experience.** Nothing in the book is hypothetical; I have worked with it or tested it on an actual project. My project experience has led to me understanding a number of things that are not covered in typical supply planning books. In this book, I pass on this understanding to you.

3. **Saturate the book with graphics.** Roughly two-thirds of a human's sensory input is visual, and books that do not use graphics—especially educational and training books such as this one—can fall short of their purpose. Graphics have also been used consistently and extensively on the SCM Focus website.

Important Terminology

This book will use a variety of terminology that it is necessary to know in order to understand the book. These terms are divided into different categories.

The SCM Focus Site

As I am also the author of the SCM Focus site, http://www.scmfocus.com, the site and the book share a number of concepts and graphics. Furthermore, this book contains many links to articles on the site, which provide more detail on specific subjects. This book provides an explanation of how supply and production planning software works, and aims to continue to be a reference after its initial reading. However,if your interest in supply planning software continues to grow,the SCM Focus site is a good resource to which articles are continually added.

The SCM site dedicated specifically to supply planning is

http://www.scmfocus.com/supplyplanning

Intended Audience

This book is for anyone interested in understanding safety stock and service levels better and particularly how to improve how they are set. This could be students or those working in companies at the operational level that will actually be making safety stock and service level improvements. It may also be of interest to consultants looking for far better ways of setting safety stock and service levels for their clients.

Another group that can benefit from the book is those in Sales. From this book, Sales can learn how unnecessary it is to guess when it comes to service levels and how the service levels can actually be quantified; but it means accepting the fact that some service levels should be set lower than they may think – it means taking a broader view which is more sustainable than simply setting all service levels at unattainable levels. This approach to service levels can create cooperation between Sales and Supply Chain rather than what is more common - conflict between the groups.

The book also should be of interest to anyone that works in supply chain management systems – both ERP and external planning systems. A final group that could benefit from the book would be those that manage supply chain departments. If you have any questions or comments on the book, please e-mail me at shaunsnapp@scmfocus.com.

Abbreviations
A listing of all abbreviations used throughout is provided at the end of the book.

Corrections
Corrections and updates, as well as reader comments, can be viewed in the comment section of this book's web page. If you have comments or questions, please add them to the following link:

http://www.scmfocus.com/scmfocuspress/supply-books/safety-stock-and-service-levels/

CHAPTER 2

Safety Stock and Service Levels from a Conceptual Perspective

A good place to start is by discussing what safety stock actually is. Safety stock is the portion of the overall stocking position that is designed specifically to **account for variability in forecasting and variability in supply**. The larger the variability in either supply or demand, the higher the proportion of safety stock to the TSL. A PLC with zero variability in demand and supply would have a safety stock of zero.

Notice that safety stock is not required because of lead-times or because of the volume of a forecast – it is because of the **variability** of either of these two components. The second most important thing to understand about safety stock is that variability is projected –it is probabilistic and therefore subject to error. If the variability was predictable, a lower level of safety stock could be maintained – however, variability is generally not predictable.

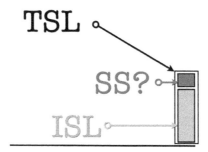

TSL, or target stocking level, is the overall target that is set by the system. Safety stock, on the other hand, is simply the specialized subcomponent of the TSL quantity that accounts for the variability in supply and demand.

The State of Safety Stock

Safety stock is greatly misunderstood and misused in industry where the failures with respect to safety stock setting are multi-dimensional. Not only are the initial calculations often of quite poor quality, but also the initially-calculated values are often managed in a highly capricious manner. One thing to understand about safety stock is that it is an operational control, **not** an executive control on the stocking level and the service level. Executives set the overall objectives and financial allocations and objectives of the company.

Safety stock needs to be set by the operators of the business - or those close to product management and planning and by those with a knowledge of inventory management. As soon as executives begin to interfere in safety stock in order to meet short-term financial objectives, the company's supply chain is essentially "toast."Actually, this same rule applies to anyone manipulating safety stock that is not accountable for the overall inventory and service level of the product location database. As an example, if a sales person can manually change the safety stock levels for their products, this is often a problem. If an individual in a factory can change the safety stock values for the products that relate to their factor, a similar bias is often entered into the system.

Service Level From the Conceptual Perspective

The service level is essentially the attempt to match demand with a certain capacity at a certain level. In supply chain management, there are two different widely used measurements of service level that are commonly used. One is referred to as order fill, which is the percentage of orders that are filled at 100%. In terms of their calculation, if 100 orders are taken and 10 of them are partially filled, the order fill rate is 90%. However, let us look at a scenario where the order fill is 90% in order to calculate the unit fill rate.

Service Level Calculator

					Orders					
	1	2	3	4	5	6	7	8	9	10
Units Per Order	25	10	10	15	20	5	5	10	20	25
Units Fulfilled	25	10	5	10	20	5	5	10	15	25
Shortage	0	0	5	5	0	0	0	0	5	0

Order Fill Rate	70%
Unit Fill Rate	90%

Here we can see the order fill rate is much higher than the unit fill rate. The order fill rate is calculated by how many times there is a shortage in an order, divided by the total number of orders. Here we have three of our ten periods with a shortage, so the order fill rate is 70%. However, when we calculate the unit fill rate, we simply divide the total number of units fulfilled by the units ordered, which comes to 90%. Typically the order fill rate is lower than the unit fill rate.

Service Level Calculator

					Orders					
	1	2	3	4	5	6	7	8	9	10
Units Per Order	25	10	10	15	20	5	5	10	20	25
Units Fulfilled	25	10	10	15	20	5	5	10	0	25
Shortage	0	0	0	0	0	0	0	0	20	0

Order Fill Rate	90%
Unit Fill Rate	86%

Here, the unit fill rate is lower than the order fill rate. The only way that this can happen is if there are few large stock-outs over the measured period.

Various people in companies will switch the usage between order fill rate and unit fill rate, with sales often preferring to use the former. However, safety stock is generally set based upon **unit fill rate**. Inventory planning systems plan in quantities, and **not normally by** specific orders. Therefore, when I refer to the service level in most of this book, I am referring to the **unit fill rate**.

The Surprising Conclusion Regarding How Service Levels are Set

The great surprise, for me anyway, regarding service levels is that even though they are quite commonly discussed, they tend to be quite arbitrarily set. The question of how to set service levels is an extremely common one within companies. Most software, even inventory management or supply planning software, assumes that the service level is known and is simply an input, when in fact companies themselves, while desiring a "high" service level, do not know what it should be - as either an average for their entire product location database or for an individual product or location. One cannot afford to have a 99% service level for all products, as it is not economical. This is shown by the following graphic:

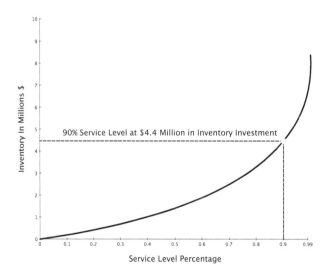

The relationship between inventory and service levels is non-linear; i.e. higher and higher service levels require disproportionate increases in inventory to support them. The closer service levels come to 100%, the more extreme the costs become.

This relationship is one of the best-documented relationships in supply chain management. The steepness of the curve above changes depending upon the safety stock formula used, as well as the increments of service level shown. Understand also that any relationship like the one shown in the graphic above holds for a certain number of input assumptions. For instance, if the forecast error were to decline, the costs of maintaining very high service levels would decrease rapidly. If the lead-times and/or the variability in lead-time decreases a great deal, the costs would decrease a great deal.

Often, strategy consultants propose that the answer to these things is simply to **change** the assumptions, so they recommend working with suppliers to bring the lead-times down or investing in a forecast improvement project to improve forecast accuracy.

The problem with many high-level consultants is that they tend to recommend making changes to inventory before these improvements in the assumptions are made. What they don't seem to acknowledge is that many of these constraints exists for a reason, and they require substantial inputs of energy and resources to change – and most are far less changeable than often proposed.

This is, in my experience, simply a way of proposing illusory improvements, and not accepting the basic limitations of the supply chain. If these things can be done, then by all means do them. However, an answer to the problem which simply changes all of the assumptions is not really answering the problem, it is evading the problem.

Forecast accuracy can almost always be improved from the current level – at least that is what my consulting experience has shown me. However, it also takes work. Lead-times can sometimes be decreased, but the degree to which they can be decreased is usually small. For instance, is the company willing to move towards more expedited shipping in order to achieve shorter lead-times? The more one investigates these things, the more apparent it becomes that making many of the changes recommended by strategy consultants simply means shifting the costs to new areas.

Why Things Don't Change With Respect to Service Level Setting

The service level-to-cost relationship is understood and settled among academics, most supply planning and inventory management software vendors and anyone with the mathematical understanding to prove the relationship. However, the lessons to be taken from this relationship do not resonate with the majority of supply chain executives. Decades after the service level-to-inventory relationship has already been demonstrated, companies continue to hold unrealistic service level targets, which it turns out are typically not attained in the natural order of things.

How do these companies continually meet unrealistic service level objectives if these objectives mathematically cannot be met with anything approaching reasonable inventory levels? The answer is simple: **They don't actually meet them in reality**. Most companies are able to meet their service level targets only "on paper" through the use of various methods that amount to inaccurate accounting for the service levels, and there are a variety of ways to calculate service levels to make them seem higher than they actually are. It turns out that when overall service levels are analyzed, actual service levels turn out to be much lower than the estimates.

Dr. Calvin Lee, in his paper on Demand Chain Optimization, states that:

> *Studies have shown that 8.3 percent of shoppers, on average, will fail to find their product in stock. These stock-outs represent 6.5 percent of all retail sales.*
>
> *Based on these studies, the service level would be either 91.7 percent or 93.5 percent depending upon whether the service level is measured at the individual demand, or the total of all units unfulfilled, divided by total units actually sold.*

This is a far cry from the 98.0, 99.0 and 99.5 percent that clients declare to me as their achieved service levels. Whom does this fool? Of course a company may falsify its service levels for internal consumption – but this does not fool customers. One of the more interesting developments in service level tracking is the rise of third parties, like Stella Service, which track the service level of retailers. Stella Service is much like Consumer Reports in that they buy and return products and then track the service level. However, instead of measuring and rating the products or the manufacturers, they rate the retailer. The following quotation explains how they got their start.

> *"The early challenge was that we wanted to buy and return millions of dollars of products in a very consistent and objective way. That had never been done before. At first, the products were being sent to our moms and their friends. As we grew, we were able to hire secret shoppers-mostly stay-at-home moms from all over the country. We don't publicly talk about how many, but it's a significant number nationwide, who are buying and returning things from their own homes."*
> – http://www.inc.com/magazine/201404/liz-welch/stella-service-rates-your-customer-service.html

Stella Service offers a variety of information to its customers, one of the outward-facing offerings is the Stella Seal to display on their websites. However, companies can review their service statistics as well as the statistics of other companies. They even show how service is trending at a wide variety of mostly online retailers. Stella Service allows companies to check their order cycle or compare themselves in terms of shipping speeds to their competitors.

Stella Service is, as the time of publishing, still quite new and they currently only rate online retailers – however, such a service could be extremely useful for other companies. If one thing is clear regarding service levels, it is that companies should be suspicious of their own internal service level estimation.

Compounding the problem, companies often assign target service goals based upon arbitrary judgments or by simply following the historical tradition, and they fail to carefully analyze the relationship between the customer service target level and the cost of excessive stock versus shortfall.

Schizophrenic Service Level Setting

However, the story is actually worse than simply decision makers picking excessive service levels. Companies can also behave schizophrenically when it comes to the rising and falling **importance** of service level objectives over time. This is a well-known phenomenon, which I have observed at many clients, and is supported in the supply chain management literature. George Plossl has the following to say on this topic:

> *"The absence of intelligent policies relating to inventory levels also leads to a panic reaction to over-weight inventories in times of falling business activity. The usual reaction is to issue a decree that inventories must be cut by some specific amount, without regard to the requirements of the business and without full realization of the impact such cuts may have on customer service, costs and employment levels. Not only is customer service hurt, but also production rate changes caused initially by falling demand are amplified greatly by untimely and excessive inventory reductions. The reverse sequence occurs when business picks up again and crash programs are initiated to rebuild depleted inventories. Poor inventory management and production planning aggravate the effects of the business cycle. Modern society, as well as professional management, should expect and demand better performance."*

Depending upon the financial ups and downs of the company and the person setting the policy, the focus may be on inventory reduction during some periods, and at other times service levels become more highly prized. This is also explained in the following quotation:

> *"In most companies, if you try to give customers all the same great service, service declines and costs spin out of control. When this happens, management has trouble rebalancing the supply chain: the objectives swing back and forth between costs and service like a pendulum. One quarter, management focuses on reducing inventories because costs are too high; the next quarter they push for increased inventories because "the customers are screaming." – Islands of Profit in a Sea of Red Ink.*

These are common problems in companies, but I propose that all of this leads back to a central proposal of this book, that service levels that are not firmly established and supported by a mathematical linkage to how the company benefits are more likely to vacillate based upon external factors. This is true of many areas of knowledge.

For instance, prior to the human understanding of the mechanism of many physical phenomena, there was a great deal of guesswork. However, once the underlying mechanism became understood, the ineffective approaches for accounting for these phenomena could be swept away – for instance the recognition that there are scientific ways of predicting tides – the focus could be placed upon accounting for just the things that we knew made a difference.

Should Service Levels be Lowered?

Some may read this book and conclude that I am proposing lower service levels across the board. This is absolutely not the case. It is true that a main observation from a number of companies is that service levels tend to be set too high; and it is certainly true that stock-outs do negatively impact sales, as logic would indicate and also as a large amount of research supports - as attested to by the following quotation:

> *"In classic inventory models, it is common to assume that excess demand is backordered. An extensive study by Gruen et al. (2002) reveals that only 15% of the customers who observe a stock-out will wait for the item to be on the shelves again, whereas the remaining 85% will either buy a different product (45%), or visit another store (31%) or not buy the product at all (9%). Similar percentages are found by Verhoef and Sloot (2006), who conclude that 23% of the customers will delay the purchase in case of excess demand."[1] - Lost Sales Inventory Systems with a Service Level Criterion*

However, I am proposing no "philosophy" when it comes to service level. Instead, I propose that the mathematics should be arranged so that service lev-

---

[1] How much an item is back-ordered or postponed to a future period versus switched way form during the purchase period or switched away from permanently greatly depends upon a number of factors such as the brand the company has established, the relative size of the purchase, its price versus competing products, and a number of other factors.

els can be calculated for the entity. Therefore, the contention of this book is not that service levels should be arbitrarily lowered, but that **a calculation** should be able to determine the appropriate service level, which is both maximally beneficial for the company as well as in line with what the customer values and is willing to pay for.

The reason why service levels tend to be set so high, and in fact too high for the company to fund sufficient inventory or production capacity to meet, is because type of quantification of the service level, that will be fully explained further on in the book, is almost never done in companies. Part of the reason for this is a lack of understanding of how to do it – and a general unavailability of this knowledge in the consulting marketplace.

However, a second reason is organizational in nature, because the interests of Sales and Marketing are not very well aligned to the interests of the overall company. This is explained by the following quotation:

> *"Because most sales are based simply on revenues – and not all sales dollars are equally profitable (many are not profitable at all) – most companies are doomed to carry significant embedded unprofitability."*
>
> – Islands of Profit in a Sea of Red Ink

This leads to the growth of unprofitable parts of the company. This is explained by the following quotation:

> *"Nearly every company is 30 t0 40 percent unprofitable by any measure. In almost every company, 20 to 30 percent of the business is highly profitable, and a large proportion of this profitability is going to cross-subsidize the unprofitable part of the business. The rest of the company is marginal. The most current metrics and control systems (budgets, etc.) do not even show the problem or the opportunity for improvement."*
>
> – Islands of Profit in a Sea of Red Ink.

For the specific product lines, the detailed information is quite shocking.

> *"35 percent of all order lines were unprofitable. 40 percent of product lines clustered by vendor were unprofitable, and an additional 38 percent were marginal. Against all expectations, fast-moving stocked products had higher gross margin (36 percent) than slower-moving ones (34 percent), and both surpassed non-stock special and custom orders (29 percent).*

It is highly likely that many of these products had **high service levels** associated with them. This is a problem repeated at many companies. We have high service levels dictated by Sales and Marketing for products that are either marginal or actually **costing money** for the company to maintain in the catalog. One has to ask the following question:

> *"Why is supply chain making such an effort to maintain a high service level on products that the company should be either indifferent as to whether they are sold or actually better off if the product is not sold?"*

Seen through this lens, it is hopefully quite apparent why it is so important to set service levels through calculations that account for product profitability. This also leads the way to one of the easiest ways to improve the profitability of companies – and it comes down very simply to cutting the non-performing product/location combinations that the business carries.

> *"By focusing on average, or aggregate profitability, you lose this essential fact, along with the opportunity to radically increase profitability at every little cost using sharply targeted measures." -*
> *Islands of Profit in a Sea of Red Ink.*

However, focusing on improving the sales of the most profitable items **is not going to happen** if the company is focused on keeping a high service level on all the items, even those that contribute either marginally **or even negatively** to profitability.

Service Level Attainability

Finally, and this is something that should be discussed and broadly understood, setting service levels too high for the resources available for the supply chain **does not make the service levels attainable.** Stretch goals may work in inspirational football movies, but they do not work in inventory management or supply planning because inventory management is not about inspiration, but about mathematics.

In fact, stretch goals reduce the service level that can be attained at any level of investment. This is because service levels beyond what is supported by investment cause a reduction in stability, as attention is moved from one group of products to another as planners attempt to improve service levels. Frankly, unsustainable service levels are a distraction from good planning because supply chain planning operates within certain constraints. These constraints include things like the number of pallet spots available, the available inventory investment, the reliability of the selected suppliers, and the forecast error, among others.

The service level is a consequence, or an **emergent property,** of the combination of these constraints, and thus is essentially their output. This is also why the service level can be calculated rather than set with guesswork or in the abstract desired level. The best way to achieve a particular service level is not to simply declare the desired service level, but to adjust the constraints that are the properties that support the level. That will hopefully become quite clear as you progress through the book.

Conclusion

Safety stock is the portion of the overall stocking position which is designed specifically to **account for variability in forecasting and variability in supply**. Safety stock is not required because of lead-times or because of the volume of a forecast – it is because of the **variability** of either of these two components. The second most important thing to understand about safety stock is that variability is projected –it is probabilistic and therefore subject to error. If the variability was predictable, a lower level of safety stock could be maintained – however, variability is generally not predictable.

Safety stock is greatly misunderstood and misused in industry where the failures with respect to safety stock setting are multi-dimensional. Not only are the initial calculations often of quite poor quality, but also the initially-calculated values are often managed in a highly capricious manner.

The service level is essentially the attempt to match demand with a certain capacity at a certain level. Most software, even inventory management or supply planning software, assumes that the service level is known and is simply an input, when in fact companies themselves, while desiring a "high" service level, do not in fact know what it should be - as either an average for their entire product location database or for an individual product or location.

Most companies are able to meet their service level targets only "on paper" through the use of various methods that amount to inaccurate accounting for the service levels, and there are a variety of ways to calculate service levels to make them seem higher than they actually are. Companies can also behave schizophrenically when it comes to the rising and falling **importance** of service level objectives over time.

An important take away from this chapter is understanding that I propose that the mathematics should be arranged so that service levels can be calculated for the entity - not that service levels should be arbitrarily lowered, but that **a calculation** should be able to determine the appropriate service level, which is both maximally beneficial for the company as well as in line with what the customer values and is willing to pay for.

Service levels should never be "stretch goals," but instead should be based upon attainable service levels given the investment in inventory and the capabilities of the company. Service levels should be set in a way that is that is considerate of the constraints in the system. These constraints include things like the number of pallet spots available, the available inventory investment, the reliability of the selected suppliers, and the forecast error, among others.

CHAPTER 3

The Common Ways of Setting Safety Stock

Safety stock is set in a variety of ways in companies. It is often set by judgment methods, like manual approximation or with averaging – such as with day's supply - or with more complex formulae like dynamic safety stock. In this chapter, I will cover all of the commonly used ways of setting safety stock that I have come across in my consulting experience and provide an explanation of how each method is used and its effectiveness.

Manual Approximation

Safety stock is often set in companies by simply allowing individuals to guesstimate what the safety stock value should be and then providing them with the rights to make the safety stock adjustments. Sometimes, the manual approximation is performed with the broader interests of the product location database in mind, but often manual approximation is performed by an individual with a bias towards a particular item or a particular group of items.

How Manual Approximation Works in Practice

I have never seen manual approximation work very well – and one of the primary reasons for this is that the person making these manual changes most often does not understand how safety stock fits into inventory management. I have witnessed safety stock being set by individuals in Sales. However, Sales has a bias to maintain more inventory than Supply Chain does because they want to set the inventory at a level that maximizes sales. Secondly, Sales tends to not have a global view.

Firstly, salespeople are generally not aware of how much it costs to maintain inventory, nor are they held accountable for the inventory level. However, they are compensated on their sales revenue, which in turn depends upon having the time to sell – so Sales has a strong bias to increase inventory whenever possible.

Secondly, there is a great deal of competition between salespeople, so Sales is really a group of competing individuals that are managed by a central overseer. That is, if one salesperson is responsible for selling some items, they may simply increase the safety stock for their items and not worry about how this affects the stocking levels of other items. Companies only have so much money to put into inventory, so if they over-allocate inventory to one set of PLCs, they must under-allocate to other PLCs. However, salespeople normally only consider how the inventory levels that are set affect "their products."

I believe the reason that planners and other supply chain planning professionals tend to focus on safety stock is not because of formal training or reading about the topic, but because it is one of the few inventory values easily altered in almost all supply planning systems. Absent a foundational understanding of the topic, people have a strong tendency to base their views on what they can control.

This is reminiscent of the story about the man who was looking in the street for his keys one night. When asked where he lost them, he replied, "On the other side of the street." Why was he looking on the wrong side of the street? Because "the light is better over here."

In the same way, even though safety stock is not a good inventory value to adjust manually, it is frequently adjusted simply because it is a convenient way of controlling the stock level within many systems. This causes problems, as safety stock is simply the portion of overall stock allocated specifically to variability.

Stock levels should **not be** controlled by manually adjusting the safety stock. Instead, safety stock should be dynamically calculated and automated, and only changed as a result of changes in the variability of supply or demand. When this is done, it is called "dynamic safety stock," and this functionality is now common in both ERP and APS systems. The standard safety stock formula resolves part of the problem; but it is an incomplete solution, as will be explained in detail further on in the book.

Even though there is ample evidence that allowing manual approximation of safety stock does not lead to good inventory and service level outcomes, it continues to be a very common way to set safety stock. A primary reason for this is that many companies don't feel as if there is a "right answer" when it comes to safety stock. However, there are far better ways to set it; they just may not happen to be some of the common ways that are explained to people.

Day's Supply Combined With a Fixed Value
Currently the most commonly used and successful way of setting safety stock is to use a combination of a day's supply combined with a fixed value.

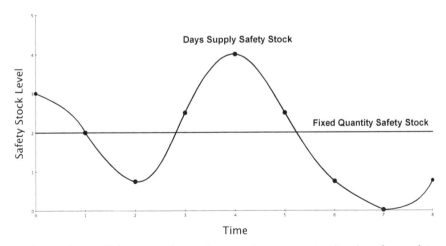

This approach works well because it varies, an important criterion for safety stock, but it does so in a way that is relatively easy to set. Essentially, this is a minimum/maximum way of setting safety stock. The day's supply value is the maximum. This changes

with the forecast. So if the forecast is 100 units for a week, and the day's supply is 3 days, then the safety stock value would be 3/7 * 100 or 42.85, rounded to 43 units.

However, due to the downward variability in some forecasts, day's supply will not work by itself; this is why blending it with a lower set value prevents the safety stock from dropping too low. However, with the upper level taken care of by day's supply, not a great deal of effort is required to calculate the minimum value.

Days' Supply Safety Stock Calculator

		Setting	Mon	Tue	Wed	Thur	Fri	Sat	Sun	Mon	Tue	Wed
	Forecast		25	10	2	0	5	5	35	45	40	65
A	Days' Supply Calculation	3 Days	37	12	7	10	45	85	120	150		
B	Minimum Safety Stock	20	20	20	20	20	20	20	20	20	20	20
	Resulting Safety Stock	Max(A,B)	37	20	20	20	45	85	120			

Here is an example of how day's supply works in detail. Along the time horizon that is represented in the image above, this is the 3-day forward-looking day's supply safety stock calculation.

The Resulting Safety Stock value simply takes the maximum of the Day's Supply Calculation and the Minimum Safety Stock. During periods of average to high forecasts, the Day's Supply Calculation ends up setting the safety stock. However on the black periods, when the forecast is low, the Minimum Safety Stock sets the actual Resulting Safety Stock value.

Therefore, the company can meet the demand in the average to high periods and also keep enough safety stock when the forecast dissipates. Safety stock should not perfectly track with the forecast, because safety stock is a buffer, and the forecast, as well as the supply, has variability or error.

This is a standard functionality in many ERP systems. However, I have actually seen the functionality decline when one moves from ERP to an advanced planning system. This is explained in the following quotation from SCM Focus on the topic of using the SNP optimizer for a client that moved from the far less sophisticated SAP ECC ERP system:

*The SM (combined safety stock day's supply and minimum safety stock value) Safety Stock Method does not work with the optimizer. This means that companies that currently use the optimizer must understand that they must use either the Safety Stock that is hard-coded into the Material Master or the Safety Time, but the system **will not use either of the two**.*

The way to approach this is to set only the Safety Stock quantity or the Days of Supply. If only the Safety Stock quantity is entered into the Material Master then the Safety Stock Method will change to SB, while if only the Days of Supply is used then the Safety Stock Method in APO becomes SZ. This would mean using the mass maintenance transaction to change every location/product combination in ERP to hold only a Safety Stock Quantity or a Days Supply.

However, there is more to this than simply the master data change. When analyzing this for one project it was working on, it was brought up that the current Safety Stock Quantities had been setup on the low side because they were designed really only to protect the lower end of the range, and essentially the Safety Stock Quantities were developed to work with the Days of Supply, or designed to work with the SM Safety Stock Method. Once Days of Supply is taken out of the equation for certain Location Products, which the Safety Stock Quantity would have to be increased. This of course requires that the business go through and increase these Safety Stock Quantities to the appropriate levels if the Days of Supply is never used.

How Day's Supply With Fixed Value Works in Practice

This approach works very well for many companies because it accounts for variability but also prevents the safety stock from falling away during periods of low demand. This method lacks sophistication and is significantly less desirable than the method of setting safety stock that will be described in Chapter 8. However it is, I believe, the most successful broadly-used approach to safety stock setting.

The Dynamic Safety Stock

The basic concept of the dynamic safety stock calculation is to adjust the safety stock per multiple factors. Often the explanation of dynamic safety stock is that it is to adjust for both supply and demand variability - as is expressed in the graphic below:

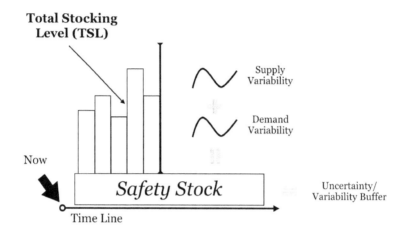

This is the dynamic safety stock formula:

Safety Stock: {Z*SQRT(Avg. Lead-time*Standard Deviation of Demand^2 + Avg. Demand^2*Standard Deviation of Lead-time^2}

This formula multiplies the average lead-time by the squared standard deviation of demand. It then takes the squared average demand and multiplies it by the squared standard deviation of lead-time. It then contains the following components:

1. *The Square Root Component:* Take the square root of the product of the primary values.

2. *The Service Level Component:* Multiply this value by "Z" which is the number of standard deviations above the mean that are determined by the inverse of the normal distribution of the service level.

This calculation is straightforward until one gets to step 2, which is the service level component. The reason for this is explained below.

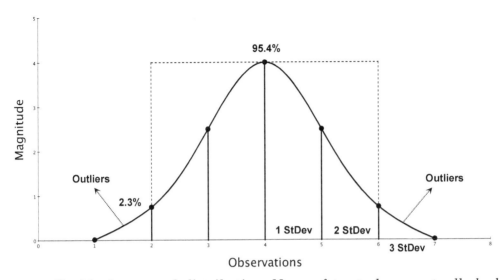

Let's start off with the normal distribution. Now safety stock can actually be based upon any probability distribution, but it is normally based upon the normal distribution. The logic is that the variance will be normally distributed. If the errors are not normally distributed, for instance in the case of service parts, then another probability distribution should be used. However, let's begin by reviewing the normal distribution above. You can see that **95.4%** of the values would fall within two standard deviations of the mean. However, this leaves areas on **both sides of the normal distribution uncovered** - and we want to cover all the possible options, all the way up to the second standard deviation to the right of the mean. Therefore the actual values we want to cover by setting the safety stock are the following:

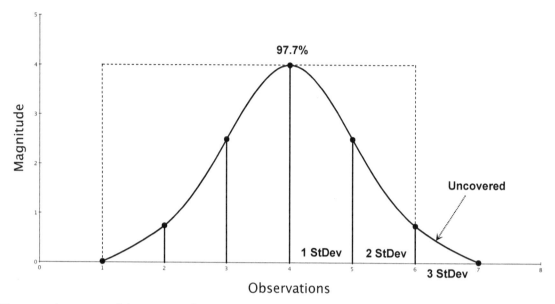

*By covering everything up to the second standard deviation up from the mean, we end up covering 97.7% of the predicted possible occurrences. The graphic above is **not a** high-detail graph, because there are more standard deviations above the second standard deviation.*

*For instance, three standard deviations to the right of the mean covers **99.9%** of all of the predicted occurrences. This level of service is never attained in supply chain management. Therefore, the service level can be converted into a standard deviation, which can then be used to multiply the values that result from step 2 in the formula steps listed above. If the desired service level is **96%**, then the standard deviation to use the safety stock formula is **1.75**. A desired service level of **98%** would use a standard deviation of **2.05** in step 3 of the safety stock formula.*

When people write about dynamic safety stock, they tend to not discuss the validity of the formula, but instead tend to quickly discuss its features. For instance, they point out that the dynamic safety stock calculation adjusts across the dimensions of service level, lead-time, and forecast error both in variability (in terms of lead-time and forecast error) as well as lead-time duration. This formula can be used to model the inventory and supply chain of an entire company. That is, instead of entering the values for a single SKU, the overall or average values can be used to help see the relationships between things like service level and the total amount of stock carried. The dynamic safety stock formula has been around for quite some time and has been incorporated into many applications with supply planning functionality. However, what is very rarely discussed is how dynamic safety stock actually works when deployed in a company.

How Dynamic Safety Stock Works in Practice

The easiest part of dynamic safety stock to understand is the service level or Z value. This is simply a probability multiplier, which assumes a normal distribution of occurrences. However, the rest of the formula is much less understandable. The following questions should be asked:

1. Why is it correct to square the values that are squared?

2. Why should the lead-time be multiplied by the forecast error or standard deviation of demand and vice versa?

The formula seems appropriately authoritative, but the more time I have spent working with the formula, the less the formula has made any sense to me. One of my major issues with those that propose the use of the standard dynamic safety stock formula is the assumption often made that the formula has been **proven in industry**, where the primary evidence for this is that the formula has been around for a long time.

However, the reality is just the opposite. The formula is little used in industry, and I could find no research papers that even tested whether the standard dynamic safety stock formula was used **or broadly successful**. I can say from my consulting experience that it is generally unused, although companies often attempt to use it. They often read about the benefits of the standard dynamic safety stock formula in a book or from a consultant, neither of which may have ever extensively tested the formula.

They then learn that the standard dynamic safety stock formula is **already available** within their supply planning application. But companies are normally unaware that few successful implementations of the dynamic safety stock formula exist. Very quickly the conversation moves to how great it would be to implement the dynamic safety stock, and the formula also provides the company with the feeling that they are moving to the leading edge by implementing this approach.

In investigating this formula, I found that explanation of dynamic safety stock is difficult to obtain. Upon review of the available safety stock calculation spreadsheets available from the Internet, I found all of them to be seriously deficient in **not fully explaining** the formula. Almost every one of the calculators asked for a service level input, but did not even explain the definition of the service level calculation definition to be used. How any person is supposed to use the online calculator reliably without knowing the correct units of measure to use is beyond me.

The vast majority of these online calculators **ignored** the lead-time component of the formula and only provided input for sales/forecast variability (error). This is **not a good way** to explain how dynamic safety stock works. Interestingly, those that left out part of formula did not even explain that it was left out - giving any person who is trying to understand the entire formula a problem. It seems as if many people want to talk about dynamic safety stock, but essentially **no one** was interested in making a clear calculator that explains safety stock.

Furthermore, there is a broader problem with the formula in that most of the explanations are not specific enough as to what the author or creator is referring to. For instance, what is "Average Demand?" Without knowing the duration that applies to the average demand, this does not mean very much. Is this the average over lead-time? The monthly average? The yearly average? Various online safety stock calculators are available at SCM Focus at the following link.

http://www.scmfocus.com/supplyplanning/2014/04/08/safety-stock-calculator/

A reverse safety stock calculator is also available at this link.

http://www.scmfocus.com/supplyplanning/2014/04/10/reverse-dynamic-safety-stock-calculation/

Conclusion

From my consulting experience, I have concluded that there is clearly a major opportunity with respect to safety stock within companies. None of the common approaches used (Manual Approximation, Days' Supply Combined with a Fixed Value, Dynamic Safety Stock, etc.) are particularly good at managing safety stock.

Of the current methods, the day's supply with fixed value approach, which is the most effective that I have seen used, is still substantially inferior to a safety stock calculation method that takes into consideration much more than simply demand combined with a lower limit to prevent the safety stock from declining too significantly when demand declines. Although there is nothing to prevent the days' supply method from being used along with an external calculator. This is where the minimum safety stock is set by the external calculator and the upper limit is set by the days' supply.

CHAPTER 4

Common Issues with Safety Stock Setting

There are many issues that prevent safety stock from being managed effectively. Here is a sample of the reasons I have found that safety stock tends not be set particularly well, at least for many companies:

1. *Poor Safety Stock Knowledge:* Safety stock with appropriate levels is not well understood. However, this is a problem that generalizes to supply chain management overall.

2. *Treating the Safety Stock as a Parameter to be Adjusted at Will:* As has been discussed, many companies manipulate their safety stock manually at will as they want more or less stock. This is done because safety stock is so easy to change. However, this is not how safety stock should be used. Safety stock should be reviewed for changes periodically, not used as a lever to adjust inventory. Secondly, when it is changed, it should be as part of a policy that affects many product/location combinations, not simply a single product location/combination.

3. *The Vendor Presentation of Safety Stock Functionality:* Most software vendors that have safety stock functionality present their functionality as leading edge. However, few applications have effective ways for setting safety stock. MEIO software is one of the few that does, but MEIO software is only implemented at a minority of companies. Safety stock determination methods, such as the standard dynamic safety stock formula, which is not very common in systems with supply planning functionality, do not actually work very well in practice – as is explained in Chapter 3. This leads some companies to the conclusion that using any system or any formula to calculate safety stock will result in poor outcomes, when this is not actually true.

I should point out that I do not see this situation changing anytime soon. This is why I would recommend that companies have their inventory parameters, such as safety stock, tuned by outside parties. However, finding an outside party that has the knowledge to set the safety stock correctly is a tricky proposition. In my interactions with a variety of vendors and consultants over the years, my view is that the consultants in the MEIO vendors have the best knowledge of how safety stock should be set.

However, those consultants are in the business of installing MEIO applications, and generally do not simply perform short-term parameter-tuning projects of this nature. However, using the calculations provided by most supply planning applications is not a very good solution. Safety stock should be viewed as a value that is tuned along with other master data parameters for supply planning, calculated externally from supply planning systems and then uploaded to these systems.

Safety Stock Setting for Input and Output Products

Companies have a lot of questions with regards to safety stock, and many of them they cannot typically answer internally. One example of this is a question I sometimes get as to whether safety stock needs to be held for raw materials and components as well as finished goods. Some seem to think that placing safety stock at both locations is redundant. In fact, a number of inventory experts believe this. The following quotation is illustrative of this viewpoint:

"The primary purpose of safety stock is to provide cushions against fluctuations in demand (forecast error) and supply (upsets in production). Demand for raw materials and components are calculated by MRP and therefore, are not subject to forecast errors. Experience with safety stock in MRP has shown clearly that the cushions are rarely found on items affected by users, nor are they large enough to be useful.

Better understanding of the importance of smooth, fast flow of materials and flexibility of operations led to the realization that the causes of upsets had to be eliminated. Efforts to do this proved successful and yielded enormous benefits far beyond the costs in incurred. Safety stock is properly only to inventory items subject to independent demand. These include stocked finished products, service parts and MPS end items....(safety stocks) **should not be duplicated at raw materials and component levels**.

Another function of safety stock is protection against uncertainly of supply. It can be useful sometimes on an item whose supply is erratic and beyond the control of people in the plant, characteristic of some purchased items. Safety stock will be wasted when production of manufactured items is erratic and unpredictable; planning cannot be sound in chaotic environments."

– Orlicky's Material Requirement's Planning

So the synopsis of this quotation is that safety stock should only be carried at the finished good location. It sounds logical; however, I think it's incorrect. The view point expressed in the quotation is more based upon a philosophy than the details of how variation is perceived at each stocking location. When looking at this second way, I believe it is clear that safety stock should be maintained in both places (the raw material and the finished good) because **each location has supply and demand variability**, as well as a lead-time – in this case the manufacturing lead-time. However, the question of how much to maintain at each location very much depends upon the scenario. The following graphic demonstrate how the amount of safety stock held at each location changes:

Safety Stock Locations

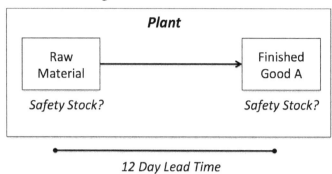

In this example, we have a one-to-one relationship between the raw material and the finished good. This is actually an important question to ask – but we will get to that in a minute. Because the lead-time is 12 days, there is not really an opportunity to carry safety stock more heavily for the raw material in order to make up for having very little of the finished goods material. This is because if demand exceeds the forecast, it will take 12 days to produce the stock if the finished goods location has its safety stock depleted. This is a perfect example of how each material requires its own safety stock.

However, by changing the assumptions, we can look at the opposite scenario in the following graphic:

Safety Stock Locations

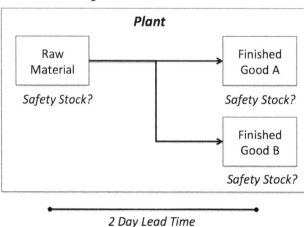

Now we have one raw material that supports two finished goods. This fact begins to switch the advantage to carrying more safety stock of the raw material, because it can support two products. This is actually a conservative example, because many compa-

nies have just a few raw materials or a few components that support quite a few finished goods. Companies that have this condition in the extreme can operate as assemble-to-order; that is, they can order the raw materials and build sub-assemblies with the knowledge that some finished good is likely to consume that material.

When this is possible, this leads to more efficient supply chain management than companies that must operate as purely make-to-stock (i.e. they must take a chance and product some finished goods that may sit, while they could have allocated production capacity to product materials that would have sold). For the vast majority of companies that speak of moving to make-to-order environments (generally the Nirvana of all companies for supply chain management), what they are actually referring to is moving to assemble-to-order.

If we return to the topic of where to store the safety stock, while being able to supply two or more finished goods from one raw material is advantageous, the only reason it is possible to carry a higher safety stock – or should I say transition the safety stock which accounts for variability at the finished good to the safety stock of the raw material - is because the lead-time is only two days. This means that, unlike the first example, if the finished goods deplete their safety stock, it is a short wait until the raw material can be converted into a finished good.

CHAPTER 5

Common Issues with Service Level Setting

Service levels are frequently discussed within companies and are of great interest to Sales, Supply Chain, and senior executives. Companies often take great pride in their service levels. However, a closer inspection of service levels, which was explained in Chapter 2, reveals the following issues are common to service level setting:

1. *Setting the service levels close to uniform for each product location*

2. *Service level attainment fudging*

3. *A lack of ability to calculate service levels based upon input factors*

4. *A misimpression of the customer service level requirement*

5. *No ability to see the inventory costs of various service levels*

6. *The setting of service levels without an attempt to manage the service level*

Each of these issues is elaborated upon in detail in the following sections.

Issue 1: Setting the Service Levels Close to Uniform for Each Product Location

One of the best pieces of evidence that a company really has no idea how to perform service level setting is if a uniform, or close to uniform, service level is applied to its products. Products are simply too varied to make this strategy work. As has been described already, companies often have marginal business lines. There is simply no way that a marginal business line should have the same, or similar, service level to the business lines that are the most profitable for the company. Marginal business lines are sometimes driven by marketing and sometimes driven by the need to consume excess production capacity. This is explained in the following quotation:

> "Some managers argue that it is a good idea to accept business that contributes, even marginally, to covering overhead. However, when you take on a lot of business that contributes only marginally to overhead, in almost all cases it will absorb a significant amount of sales and operations resources that otherwise would have been devoted to increasing your "good" business. And it will remain and grow into the embedded profitability that drags down earnings in company after company. If the underlying reason for taking marginal business is to fill unused capacity, you need a sunset policy to stop taking the marginal business once capacity is filled and to remove it when full freight business is available. Not many companies have the information and discipline to do this."
>
> – Islands of Profit in a Sea of Red Ink

Therefore a good service level strategy is one that is differential; that is, the service levels change depending upon the product and the product location – at the very least. Other differential settings can be applied to customers. This is considered the Holy Grail by Sales and Marketing, but it is tricky to implement as most often customers do not have dedicated stocking locations, and supply planning systems calculate the service level at a specific product location – not for a customer.

Issue 2: Service Level Attainment Fudging

Most companies do not achieve anywhere close to the service levels that they say or think they do. This is because there are a variety of ways to improve service levels by removing occurrences. One of the most popular of these is to **eliminate products** that are back-ordered from the service level calculation.

Issue 3: A Lack of Ability to Calculate Service Levels Based Upon Input Factors

I have alluded to the fact that service levels are most often arbitrarily set in supply chain management; however, in performing research for this book I found that service levels are often also arbitrarily set for IT services. This is explained in the following quotation:

> *"However, in practice and in academia, up to now, there is no commonly accepted engineering approach to determine business relevant performance metrics (service level indicators) and associated cost efficient target values (service level objectives) to precisely define service level quality. We illustrate this deficit using the example of IT services. In practice, service level indicators and service level objectives for IT services are often determined in an ad-hoc and heuristic way, which is sometimes even referred to as "pure guesswork." In addition, the current process used to define SLIs and SLOs often lacks the end user business perspectives."*
> – Hawaii International Conference of System Services, 2011.

This, as well as other sources, points to the fact that service level setting is really a problem in **multiple areas**. I believe all of these problems with respect to service level setting have a similar root cause - the inability to calculate service levels based upon objective supporting variables.

Issue 4: A Misimpression of the Customer Service Level Requirement

There are two very interesting observations regarding service level with respect to the impression of customer service levels:

1. Most of those that specialize in setting service level targets within companies don't actually know what service levels should be set to maximize profits.

2. Most customers do also not know what service level they need.

Higher service levels are often requested for customers to make up for previous service failures. Remember that, as explained in Chapter 2, companies do not normally meet the service levels they set for themselves. This is a major point of denial for companies, but their customers certainly know that they do not meet the promised service levels. This sets up a feedback loop where customers ask for increasingly high service levels, which Sales and Marketing use as evidence that the company must further increase service levels. This is explained in the following quotation:

> *"There are two problems with simply asking the customer what order cycle he or she requires (this author uses the term "order cycle" instead of service level). First, the customer may not know his or her real needs, especially in companies where the purchasing group is separate from the operations group. In the absence of this understanding, it is safest for the customer's purchasing staff to simply demand faster and faster service. Second, most customers will ask for shorter and shorter order cycles if they don't trust the vendor to keep its delivery promises. In fact, all products require flawless service levels, but different products need different order cycles."*
> – Islands of Profit in a Sea or Red Ink

In this way, inflated service levels are used as a proxy for lower service level variability. Again, most companies incorrectly measure their own service levels. So if a company thinks it is providing a 98% service level, when it is in fact it is providing a 92% service level (which is often the case) then the fact that customers complain about the current service level is not evidence that the service level target should be moved to 98.5% or to 99%. Secondly, if a customer is unhappy with the **variability** of service level that they receive, this is not evidence that the service level should be increased.

Issue 4: No Ability to See the Inventory Costs of Various Service Levels

Most companies are not able to see or understand the interaction between service levels and the costs of maintaining a service level. The only application that does this is a MEIO application; all other supply planning applications simply treat the service levels as an input to the dynamic safety stock calculation. This builds stock, but does not show the relationship between service level and stock for implementing companies (the relationship could be extracted and placed into a graph, but it normally is not).

As a consequence, most companies think it is much less expensive to maintain very high service levels than it actually is. Therefore, the most common scenario is for high service level targets to be set, service level targets **that are unattainable** given the company's forecast error and its inventory investment, and then to **fudge meeting the targets**.

Sales will often try a variety of techniques to push the service level higher than is sustainable. One way is to create forecasts that are higher than what they actually will sell. Another is to actively go into the supply planning system and increase the safety stock. Because the Sales team is most often setup as a group of competing individuals, who are all trying to meet separate sales quotas, if individuals in the team can allocate more inventory to their particular products, at the expense of products that are assigned to other sales reps, they will tend to do this.

Issue 5: The Setting of Service Levels Without an Attempt to Manage the Service Level

Sales and Marketing can make life very difficult for Supply Chain and Operations by simply insisting that a large number of products be carried, that new products be perpetually introduced, and that a very high service level be maintained for all the product/location combinations. In fact, this is the dominant approach in most US companies.

However, instead of looking at Operations as simply an entity on which one places negative externalities and viewing inventory and production capacity as an infinite box from which capacity is pulled, Sales and Marketing could actually help Supply Chain manage its service levels. It could only promote those items that are well-stocked instead of running promotions independent of what is available.

Currently, there is very frequently a poor communication of basic promotion information between Sales and Marketing and Supply Chain, and in many (if not most) companies there is little substantive interacting between the two. This is covered in detail in the SCM Focus Press book *Promotions Forecasting: Techniques of Forecast Adjustments in Software*. But, more broadly, Sales and Marketing could work to not simply sell everything but to sell what is available. This is part of what is referred to as demand shaping. This is covered in the following quotation:

> *"Dell purposely selected customers with relatively predictable purchasing patterns and low service costs. The company developed a core competence in targeting customers, and kept a massive database for this purpose. A large portion of Dell's business stemmed from long term corporate accounts with predicable needs closely tied to their budget cycles. Demand management. "Sell what you have" was the phrase that Dell developed for the crucial function of matching incoming demand to predetermined supply."*
>
> – Islands of Profit in a Sea of Red Ink.

A review of Dell's process by Dr. Jonathan Byrnes reveals that Dell had a true S&OP process where *"they revised the company's sales targets and production plan to reflect Dell's evolving situation"* and *"sales commission plan was set to equal the production plan."* The effect of all of this was to enable Sales and Supply Chain to actually play for the same team, unlike in most companies where Sales and Supply Chain fight against one another. In this way, Sales begins to **take responsibility for the service level** in a much more proactive way than simply setting service level goals that cannot be reached without fudging the service level measurement statistics.

Demand management is the activity of proactively controlling demand rather than simply taking orders. This improves forecast accuracy and reduces inventories. However, in most companies, not only is demand management not practiced, but through promotional activities and attempting to meet various end-of-quarter sales goals, the normal variability of demand is **exaggerated**.

In every company I have consulted with, these activities convert many products that actually are forecastable into being un-forecastable. There is a serious problem when the variability of the sales history is much higher than the actual authentic demand – and for most companies it almost always is. In this way, this "demand wrecking" is a primary reason that forecasting is so much more difficult than it needs to be.

The Root Cause of These Issues

Overall, even with all the technology at our disposal, service levels are set in an unsophisticated manner. When service levels are simply a matter of opinion, which they are in most companies, it becomes very difficult to come to a rational conclusion as to what service levels should be. For instance, one of the very common assumptions is that a company should have a blanket service level. That is either one service level or a very narrow range of service levels.

Why is this assumption so uncritically accepted? Even without having a great deal of supply chain expertise, it should be self-evident that some products or product lines may be much higher margin than other product lines. Setting a high service level for all products may sound like a worthy goal, but it means that the higher margin items end up **subsidizing** the service levels of the lower margin items.

A question that is often missing in discussions of service level setting is: What does the customer actually value? That does not mean *What does the company think the customer values*, but what do they *actually* value? If a customer is willing to pay the premium for a very high service level then they, by definition, value it. If they are not willing to do this, then they probably do not value it.

The next logical question is: Should the company make investments in inventory and service level that the customer is not willing to pay for? The question would seem to answer itself. The intent should be to match the service level that the customer wants.

If a company is setting service levels that are continually set to a level that is too high for the customer's preferences, the company will naturally need to charge more for the product – and this increase in price may limit sales. Therefore, an intelligent discussion on service level will begin with the assumption that a number of factors affect the sales of a product – and service levels and costs will move in **opposite directions**. Tuning both to the desires of the customer will lead to the best possible outcome for the company.

There are certain environments where service levels simply must be very high. The following quotation from a research paper on service levels describes these environments well:

> *"Decision makers with stock-out adverse preferences have a strong interest in strict service level policies. These policies are particularly needed for supply chains operating in highly competitive, military, or humanitarian environments, those dealing with a few large dominant customers, those selling high profit products, or those in which a shortage would trigger huge costs to setup the production process all over again."*
> – Probabilistic Modeling of Multi Period Service Levels.

That is perfectly fine. There is nothing wrong with very high service levels; the problem comes in with very high service levels that are unsubstantiated.

Conclusion

In addition to lacking the right set of tools to set service levels, companies tend to repeat the same mistakes with respect to service level setting. If I could come up with one adjective to describe how I see service levels managed it would be "muddled." Most companies simply lack the ability to control their service levels and connect the service level to a level of investment or knowledge. I often see service levels declared as all-important, but how much are companies willing to invest on the knowledge side of the equation to improve service levels? It appears to be not very much.

In this chapter, I covered some of the major issues with how service levels are set and controlled. The most fundamental misunderstanding is that companies most often have little idea how much their customers value service level. Providing a service level of 98% is quite expensive under normal circumstances (the simpler the setup of the supply chain and the fewer products carried, the higher the volume, the easier it is to attain higher service levels – but most companies have difficult and overly complicated supply chains and product location combinations).

How do companies know that their customers are willing to actually pay for attaining higher service levels? There is also evidence, explained in this chapter, that higher service levels are requested in order to increase the service level over the fudged service level that is actually attained. Therefore, Sales and Marketing may request a 98% service level – with the hopes that some lower service level is attained. This could be considered a form of service level bluffing.

CHAPTER 6

Service Level Agreements

No coverage of service levels would be complete without covering service level agreements or SLAs. SLAs are methods of charging different customers different prices for different levels of service. SLAs sometimes occur in situations with products being sold, but are actually most common in IT services.

In fact, simply typing in "service level" and "white paper" into Google will find the majority of results being related to IT service SLAs. However, the principles behind an SLA are the same regardless of what the SLA is actually for. The article "Winning in the Aftermarket" in the Harvard Business Review explains SLAs well:

> *"Companies must design a portfolio of service products;*
> *different customers have different service needs even*
> *though they may own the same product. For example,*
> *when a mainframe computer in a stock exchange fails,*
> *the financial impact will be more severe than when a*
> *mainframe in a library goes down."*

SLAs began in the service or aftermarket market, but have moved into the finished goods market, as many companies increasingly want to manage their supply chains and customers by differentiated service levels. This is a very common goal for many finished goods manufacturers and distributors. SLAs have been in existence for quite some time and are very well understood as a method of managing a business.

The History of SLAs

SLAs developed as a method for guaranteeing a certain level of service for a specific level of compensation. The SLA provider is required to meet the stipulations in the contract or is required to compensate the SLA customer. SLAs have become common in all types of businesses, from telecom to aerospace and defense.

SLAs are similar to software as a solution (SaaS) in that they closely tie the incentives of the customer and the provider. In fact, SaaS subscriptions are often sold with an SLA. I once interviewed Erik Larkin at Arena Solutions, and he discussed how good things happen when the incentives of companies and customers are in alignment. When I was interviewing Erik and listening to his comments on SaaS, I immediately thought of SLAs. Although Erik Larkin and Nathan Martin are speaking of SaaS solutions in the following video, the same could be said for SLAs.

> http://www.scmfocus.com/supplychaininnovation/2010/10/eric-larkin-andnathan-martin-from-arena-solutions-on-the-benefits-of-saas/

One of the best-known and most effective users of SLAs is the networking giant Cisco. You can read about their SLA program at their website:

> http://www.cisco.com/en/US/products/ps6602/products_ios_protocol_group_home.html

While Cisco's products can be a bit obscure for those who do not work in networking, just about everyone is familiar with Google Apps. Google Apps offer both a free and paid version and, under the paid version, they offer an SLA, which you can read about below or see at their website:

Go**ogle** Apps

Businesses	**Google Apps Service Level Agreement**
Schools	Google Apps SLA. During the Term of the applicable Google Apps Agreement (the "Agreement"), the Google Apps
Organizations	Covered Services web interface will be operational and available to Customer at least 99.9% of the time in any
	calendar month (the "Google Apps SLA"). If Google does not meet the Google Apps SLA, and if Customer meets
Applications	its obligations under this Google Apps SLA, Customer will be eligible to receive the Service Credits described
Admin features	below. This Google Apps SLA states Customer's sole and exclusive remedy for any failure by Google to meet the Google Apps SLA.
Tours & demos	Definitions. The following definitions shall apply to the Google Apps SLA.
Customers	"Downtime" means, for a domain, if there is more than a five percent user error rate. Downtime is measured
Apps Marketplace	based on server side error rate.
FAQ	"Google Apps Covered Services" means the Gmail, Google Calendar, Google Talk, Google Docs, Google Groups and Google Sites components of the Service. This does not include the Gmail Labs functionality, Google Apps – Postini Services, Gmail Voice or Video Chat components of the Service.
News & events	"Monthly Uptime Percentage" means total number of minutes in a calendar month minus the number of
Contact sales	minutes of Downtime suffered in a calendar month, divided by the total number of minutes in a calendar
Support	month.
	"Service" means the Google Apps for Business service (also known as Google Apps Premier Edition), Google Apps for Government service, Google Apps for ISPs service (also known as Google Apps Partner Edition), or Google Apps for Education service (also known as Google Apps Education Edition) (as applicable) provided by Google to Customer under the Agreement.

Standard Limitations in Supply Network Control

Supply chain departments at companies are continually challenged by service level control, for two main reasons:

1. They lack the correct software to control service level the way they want.

2. They often cannot agree upon the service levels (beyond very high level goals).

It is strangely inconsistent that so many companies have so much focus on service levels, but lack the software to control service levels. Most supply planning methods lack the mechanism to control service levels the way that companies would like, requiring companies to spend an extraordinary amount of time managing service levels. These companies have service level controls, but most of these controls, such as the day's supply, are indirect.

Dynamic safety stock can only be set at the product/location combination. Service level is a critical key performance indicator (KPI) to which the bonuses of higher-ups are tied, but which can only be controlled indirectly. Without the proper control mechanism, supply chain planning becomes more reactive and execution-oriented. This is a problem at many companies. To understand this, it's important to review how the goals of supply chain organizations are set.

Directors at supply chain organizations are given different service level objectives by their vice presidents. VPs receive pressure on service level attainment from their sales organizations. The VP must keep inventories down, but must simultaneously satisfy the sales side by keeping the service levels high. Often salespeople will contact the Supply Chain director(s) and ask that a particular customer be given priority over others. These interactions may result in emails to directors needing them to "understand" how important this or that customer is to the business. The director then writes emails back stating that the sales organization must "understand" that the supply chain organization faces certain constraints.

However, as much as Sales or the Supply Chain department proposes a service level for a product location (or for a customer's product), there is no clear evidence that the customer is willing to pay for the service level requested. This means that some customers may be paying a higher price than they want to and thus are more likely to go to a competitor; this also means that some customers are paying too low of a price, depressing the profits of the company that is managing the supply chain in question. This is where SLAs come in to play.

Reducing Friction between the Sales Organization and Supply Chain

The constant friction between Sales and Operations described in the previous paragraphs is due in large measure to the fact that the incentives of sales organizations and supply chain organizations are not aligned with one another. This is true both in overall terms and among the smaller units within the organization. Much of the effort and conflict comes from determining which customers will receive priority over others.

For example, salespeople benefit more if their customers receive more inventory and a higher service level than the company's direct customers. When incentives are misaligned (and in truth Sales and Operations tend to be misaligned regardless of the company or industry), it becomes more critical to have the necessary information to quantify the key decision-making variables in order to resolve the conflict. Without a strong connection between Sales and Supply Chain/Operations, salespeople can propose that some customers are more important than others (this customer is bigger, older, or more profitable and thus deserves priority).

This is a prescription for conflict and shifting objectives, as competing interests become more or less influential over time. Thus, what often happens is that the biggest customer takes precedence. However, this is not necessarily the best decision for the company, as smaller companies may be more profitable or have other characteristics that make them better to do business with. Some companies draw no distinctions between customers, and attempt- at least on paper - to satisfy all customers at the same service level. Indeed, this may work for some companies, but other companies that could benefit from offering different service levels to different customers don't do this because they lack the tools and capabilities to do so. SLAs can certainly help in this area.

Providing a Menu of Options to Customers

The combination of SLAs and the ability to intelligently set service level-based safety stock is very empowering to the company that has the ability to accurately price new business - as this new business can be sustainably supported by the company's supply chain. SLAs, combined with the right supply chain planning tools, allow companies to provide a "menu of options" to customers like the one listed below.

Service Level		SLA Cost
95%	=	$2,854,000
92%	=	$2,290,000
87%	=	$1,830,000
85%	=	$1,512,000

A company with this type of capability can ask their prospective customer how much they would be willing to pay. Based on this information, the company can then provide the prospective customer with an estimated service level. Alternatively, the company can publish a list of service levels and costs from which the customer can choose to fit their needs.

Conclusion

SLAs are methods of charging different customers different prices for different levels of service. SLAs began in the service market, but have moved into the finished goods market, as many companies increasingly want to manage their supply chains and customers by differentiated service levels. SLAs are a way of aligning both the SLA provider and customer as well as Operations (which is concerned with costs) along with Sales and Marketing (which is concerned with revenue and normally unconcerned with costs).

Without a strong connection between Sales and Supply Chain/Operations, salespeople can propose that some customers are more important than others. Some companies draw no distinctions between customers, and attempt - at least on paper - to satisfy all customers at the same service level.

Indeed, this may work for some companies, but other companies that could benefit from offering different service levels to different customers don't do this because they lack the tools and capabilities to do so. SLAs can certainly help in this area.

A company with this type of capability can ask their prospective customer how much they would be willing to pay. Based on this information, the company can then provide the prospective customer with an estimated service level. Sounds great doesn't it? Setting up the service level contracts are the easy part. The difficult part is having the ability to perform the analysis that can allow the SLA provider to provide a reasonably accurate estimation of its costs at different service levels.

I one interviewed a person who set SLAs and negotiated with SLA customers. This person told me that because of the power dynamic, that they mostly agreed to whatever the customer was willing pay, and therefore they did not require a sophisticated approach to setting relative SLAs. This seems like a good way to lose a lot of money. Several technologies still to be discussed in this book do allow a company to take an intelligent approach to pricing SLAs.

CHAPTER 7

Safety Stock and Service Levels in Inventory Optimization and Multi-Echelon Software

The most sophisticated way to set safety stock and service levels that currently exists is with inventory optimization and multi-echelon software, known as "MEIO" for short. I have spoken briefly about MEIO throughout the book, and in this chapter we will cover MEIO in detail.

MEIO is an innovative use of two separate forms of optimization: inventory optimization and multi-echelon inventory optimization (but which I simply refer to as multi-echelon planning to reduce confusion). Each type of optimization answers separate supply chain planning questions. Unlike all other supply planning methods that divide the supply planning problem (called decomposition and explained in detail in the following article, which uses the SAP APO SNP application to explain decomposition) so that some products or locations are completely processed before other products or locations before others, MEIO decomposes the problem for every addition of stock to the supply network.

http://www.scmfocus.com/sapplanning/2011/10/12/snp-optimizer-sub-problem-division-and-decomposition/

That is how MEIO calculates the service level impact of carrying one additional item at every product/location combination and then sorts the list of options by their contribution to service levels and selects the best "contributor."

The Definition of Inventory Optimization

Inventory optimization is the derivation of stocking levels throughout the supply planning network based on service level targets. Inventory optimization answers the question of how much inventory should be carried, while, as I'll discuss later, multi-echelon answers the question of where in the supply network quantities should be carried.[1]

Unsurprisingly, these are the two most important questions in supply planning. Although all inventory optimization works this way, specifically how stocking levels are controlled by service levels depends on the individual approach of each particular MEIO vendor.

What is really quite amazing is that MEIO software does this for every product-location combination in the supply network and for every **intermediate state** between the starting inventory position until it hits either a service level or inventory investment cap (depending upon how the application is run). This **stops the model** from continuing to add inventory at a point declared within the application. A simplified version of the formula for the inventory optimization piece is shown below. Not all vendors use the same approach, but this graphic is a general approximation of how most of these applications work.

---

[1] Definitions for both inventory optimization and multi echelon planning can be found at the following links: http://www.scmfocus.com/inventoryoptimizationmultieche-lon/2010/04/inventory-optimization-definition/, http://www.scmfocus.com/inventoryopti-mizationmultiechelon/2007/08/multiechelon-definition/. For those interested in more detail on MEIO, see the SCM Focus Press book Inventory Optimization and Multi Echelon Planning Software.

Basic Decision Making Criteria

$$\text{Maximize} \left(\begin{array}{c} \text{Potential Contribution to} \\ \text{Service Level / Material} \\ \text{Cost} \end{array} \right)$$

In the example above, there are only nine options to evaluate. However, as the number of factors to be compared increases (such as the product-location combinations and the number of SKUs), the number of overall options that the model must evaluate increases very rapidly, all of which can be predicted by combinatorial mathematics.

Those who have calculated the total possible number combinations resulting from two dice being rolled have experience with exactly this type of analysis. MEIO models often have millions of options to compare in order to complete a single planning run. The model must develop a rating for every possible location combination, which it can then sort or rank, and based on this it selects the inventory transactions that will best contribute to service levels.

How Inventory Optimization Works

Inventory optimization is a subset of mathematical optimization. A solver is what computes the inventory optimization and the multi-echelon planning mathematics. The type of mathematics categorizes the optimizer. Inventory optimization and multi-echelon planning are customized forms of optimization specifically designed around the needs of supply planning. Among differences in their design approaches to solve the same problem, MEIO vendors differ substantially in terms of where the service level can be set in their applications.

Inventory optimization does not optimize the safety stock in the system, but optimizes the **target stocking level** at each product location based on a service level that can be set in a variety of locations. However, because safety stock is based on the initial stocking level, MEIO has the ability to calculate more efficient, and often lower, safety stock based on its more sophisticated modeling of the probable interactions of the locations in the supply network. Inventory optimization is effective for supply planning because it is customized for the most important business goal of many, although certainly not all, supply planning organizations: the minimization of inventory at any service level.

One of MEIO's major features is the control it gives planners and organizations over service levels. Highlighting their flexibility, MEIO applications can also start from an **inventory goal and work toward the service level**. That is they can work in "forward or reverse." This is very valuable for companies that have a hard cap on inventory dollars that they are willing to allocate. Unfortunately, it is more common to have hard caps on space versus inventory dollars, which are often allowed to fluctuate widely.

MEIO software can demonstrate the relationship of every possible combination of service level versus inventory investment and can recreate the relationship based on SKU-level modeling. This capability replicates the inventory-to-service-levels graphic that is familiar to most supply chain professionals, and does so in a way that is very precisely based upon the company's real data, making MEIO applications very powerful for simulation. In fact, several MEIO applications allow for simulation by planners and do not require any special set-up.

Now that I have provided a brief overview of MEIO, lets get into the implications of MEIO calculated safety stock.

Dynamic Safety Stock
Almost any ERP system can calculate safety stock dynamically. Alternatively, safety stock can be entered manually as a hard-coded value or calculated externally by a variety of methods -- including from MEIO. (In fact, one popular method of using the MEIO application is to export the safety stock value to the safety stock field in the ERP system.)

MEIO applications also have dynamic safety stock functionality; however, this is separate from MEIO functionality. And this is an important point, because it is often a confusing topic for companies that implement MEIO applications. The safety stock is simply calculated based upon **MEIO-derived initial stocking levels**. Inventory optimization does not optimize the safety stock, but optimizes what MCA Solutions has coined the "target stocking level" (or TSL), and does so for the entire supply network.

Safety stock, on the other hand, is calculated independently at each location product combination. Safety stock is **only a subcomponent** of the TSL. The main functionality in MEIO goes toward calculation of the initial stocking level (ISL). It is from the ISL that safety stock is derived. Combining the ISL and the safety stock derives the TSL. The relationship is as follows:

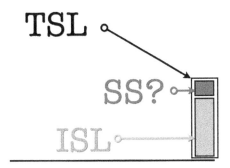

Therefore, the best way to think of TSL is as the total stock target at a product and location combination. Safety stock, on the other hand, is simply the **specialized subcomponent** of the TSL quantity that accounts for the variability in supply and demand. Safety stock calculated with an MEIO application will be lower than the safety stock calculated by any other supply planning method. However, this is not due to MEIO's inventory optimization functionality, but rather to its **multi-echelon functionality.**

Multi-echelon functionality can both see and interpret the relationships between locations that non-multi-echelon systems cannot. This is because multi-echelon functionality has the mathematics to control inventory in the system at all the locations in the supply network as interrelated. That is how the stocking level at a parent location impacts both the stocking decision and the service level at the child location.

Non multi-echelon supply planning systems use a lower level of sophistication – one which assumes that all locations are independent of another. However, this is not a correct assumption. I don't want to go too much further into why this is the case, as this is really just a brief overview of a complex technology – however for those interested in more details regarding the assumptions of location interdependence, see the following article. The secret to really understanding multi echelon planning is in understanding the concept of effective lead time.

http://www.scmfocus.com/inventoryoptimizationmultiechelon/2010/01/
effective-lead-time-and-multi-echelon/

Conclusion

MEIO is an innovative use of two separate forms of optimization: inventory optimization and multi-echelon optimization. Each answers separate supply chain planning questions. Inventory optimization answers the question of how much to keep in inventory, while multi-echelon optimization answers the question of where to keep inventory in the supply network.

Unlike supply planning techniques that use sequential processing or calculation, MEIO calculates the service level impact of carrying one additional item at every product location combination and then sorts the list of options by their contribution to service levels and selects the best contributor. Different vendors do this in different ways, and during the software selection phase, it is worthwhile to understand how the vendors on your shortlist perform this important step.

MEIO applications do this for every stocking decision and iteratively build up the stock from the first stocking decision to the last, until it arrives at an ending stocking position. This ending stocking position, which is supported by a series of transaction recommendations, is then the "supply plan."

One of MEIO's major features is the control it gives planners and organizations over service levels. Highlighting their flexibility, MEIO applications can also start from an **inventory goal and work toward the service level**. That is they can work in "forward or reverse." This is very valuable for companies that have a hard cap on inventory dollars that they are willing to allocate.

Unfortunately, it is more common to have hard caps on space versus inventory dollars, which are often allowed to fluctuate widely. I am a fan of MEIO software and even wrote a book on the topic.

However, MEIO software is probably too dominant in the discussion of service levels. This is because only a minority of companies will ever purchase an MEIO application, and for many this technology is overkill. Therefore, for other companies, there has to be a better way of calculating service levels instead of purchasing an entirely new system. One approach that I have used to good effect is explained in the following chapter.

CHAPTER 8

A Simpler Approach to Comprehensively Setting Safety Stock and Service Levels

For a number of years now, I have advised clients to stop thinking in terms of a single solution for supply planning and to entertain more than one supply planning solution- including external simulation tools and general optimization solvers - that can enhance their company's capabilities and meet more requirements that any one tool can, even with expensive enhancements. This is an unorthodox approach because the large consulting companies promote the mindset that all of the supply planning needs of a company can, and should, be met by a single application and that furthermore, no other system should be used to simulate or otherwise adjust the production systems.

Financial incentives blind many to the opportunities that exist in this regards. Software vendors consider other applications or even other calculators or tools to be a threat and are generally opposed to them. It's hard to make a general statement about all consulting companies, but certainly, the large consulting companies are tied at the hip with specific software vendors and generally propose that everything that is needed to implement and tune a system is provided by the system itself.

Generally, large consulting companies tend to serve as sales arms of the large software vendors – and don't have an independent opinion on these types of topics. When it comes to the internal IT department within implementing companies, their incentives are to limit the number of applications that are used to as few applications as possible.[1]They think that this reduces their maintenance overhead – but with respect to supply chain planning systems – they tend to greatly underestimate how a second system or external calculator can reduce the maintenance of the primary system.

For example, companies I have consulted with have gone for years unable to properly set their supply planning parameters because they bought the logic that all that is needed to setup parameters is provided by the business or in some cases can be calculated by their primary application. Running a supply planning system in such a suboptimal manner, for so many years, dwarfs the costs of using a third party system. Of course, these companies were also not aware that an external calculator, which does not require an implementation of another product, even existed.

More evidence to support my proposal is the fact that service levels and safety stock is illogically set at so many companies. This is a perfect example of the problem of putting all of one's eggs in one's basket. Companies purchase supply planning functionality in the form of ERP systems, and specialized external supply planning systems or APS systems, thinking that these systems hold the answer for improving service levels. This is part of the sales pitch on the part of the software vendors. However, there is really no supply chain application with much in the way of service level setting functionality aside from MEIO applications.

How most systems with supply planning functionality account for service levels is with dynamic safety stock functionality – which does not work in the vast majority of companies that activate this functionality. In fact, unless the company purchases an MEIO system, **nothing very much sophisticated** or particularly advantageous is available for either service level setting or safety

---

[1] However, even a single application can have too much maintenance if the application is naturally higher in maintenance.

stock calculation. However, at client after client, there does not seem to be the awareness of this that I would expect at this point.

This approach of relying upon the big system for these values has been thoroughly tested and provides suboptimal results. Companies are generally not properly informed of the capabilities of the safety stock and service level functionality when they purchase their ERP or APS system, and they can often work with the settings for years without ever figuring out that there is often nothing new in these areas over the system that they replaced.

As I stated earlier, after years of seeing this issue at my various clients, I have concluded that most companies need to calculate both service levels and safety stock **outside** of the ERP system or APS system. In terms of the information that is generally explained on this topic, only the MEIO vendors actually recommend doing this same thing – and this is under the scenario where their application is connected to the main supply planning system. An MEIO application can be run in two basic ways:

1. *As the Primary Supply Planning System:* As the primary supply planning application, it creates the purchase requisitions and the stock transfer orders that are sent to the ERP system – under this design, the MEIO application could have an inventory cap set for it, and then determine service levels as well as safety stock. In this case, planners use the MEIO system by going into its user interface and using it as any other planning system.

2. *As a Secondary System:* Here, the MEIO system performs calculations for service level and safety stock and even other values that the implementing company decides to use, and these values are then extracted from the MEIO system and uploaded to either the ERP system or the APS system. In this way, the MEIO application is leveraged to create input values that are then sent to the live supply planning system.

There are certainly advantages of running MEIO in the first way; however running an MEIO system in the second way can be expensive because it requires the implementation and maintenance of a system that is not actually live – however most MEIO systems are priced to really be the primary supply planning system. When used as a secondary system, the implementing company does obtain good quality input values for their production system, but at a relatively high cost and at a high level of complexity and long-term maintenance costs.

However, while it is important to understand MEIO technology to understand how to set service levels and safety stock, only a minority of companies will purchase MEIO systems. And MEIO systems as presently designed do not incorporate production constraints; therefore will not be attractive to many manufacturing companies. Therefore, it's important to have a strategy for service level and safety stock calculation that does not involve the implementation of a new system.

Several years ago, I thought that using an easy-to-run supply planning system would be the right approach for modeling service levels, safety stock, and other inventory parameters. I have been a proponent of what is called simulation — where a single change is made to anything in the model (say service levels) and then the model is run to see what the change is in planning output. In fact at SCM Focus, there is an entire sub-site dedicated to simulation:

  http://www.scmfocus.com/supplychainsimulation/

However, once I attempted to do this for a range of parameters, I found that the results were often inconclusive – and furthermore it was quite time consuming. The problem is that simulation takes a lot of time to run, and most planning departments don't have the resources to run many simulations. Simulation is also tricky because every change that is made to the application must be documented in terms of its affect. This is explained in the following article:

  http://www.scmfocus.com/sapplanning/2009/11/08/scm-simulation-archival-blog/

For many supply planning parameters, including all of those discussed in this book, simulation using off the shelf software (that is the software that is the primarily implemented system) is **not** the best approach for modeling things like the effect of service levels on inventory. In my experience it is far easier, and the output is far better, to calculate these values and make changes to them in an external calculator.

Another reason why an external calculator is far better is that simulation can only be performed with a change to one field, or should I say one field for either a portion of, or the entire product location database, at a time. So if we wanted to test the change tothe outcome from changes in lead-time on safety stock, the following table would show how many simulations would have to be run.

Simulation Matrix

Simulation Number	Simulation Change	Recorded Change in Average Stock Level
1	All Lead Times Reduced by 10%	
2	All Lead Times Reduced by 15%	
3	Lead Times for Group A Reduced by 20%	

This is time consuming because the change must be made to the master data each time, and then the procedure rerun and then the output recorded. Most supply planning systems make it very difficult to extract the changes in the output, which in most cases we will want to be extracted in an aggregate fashion. This is much more time consuming and less precise than using an external calculator because when using an external calculator you are not simply "poking around" trying to find areas where the output is improved – instead the calculated value directly changes from whatever input you desire changed.

In fact, an external calculator can, and should, calculate more values than this - as will be explained further on in this chapter. However, let's discuss the requirements for the calculation of service levels and safety stock.

Important Requirements for Both Service Level and Safety Stock Setting

Now that I have established the importance in the use of an external calculator in tuning the supply planning parameters of he primary system, let's discuss what should be expected from the calculator.

The following is what is required in order to effectively develop service level and safety stock values. Let us begin with the requirements for calculating safety stock:

Safety Stock Calculation Requirements

1. *Accounts for Variability:* Obviously, as safety stock is designed to account for variability in demand and supply, it should be determined in part based upon variability.

2. *Dynamic:* Dynamic means that the value is recalculated as the inputs change. A major philosophical selling point of the dynamic safety stock formula is that it changes as conditions change. While it would be optimal if the formula were dynamic, calculating the value outside of the supply planning system, which turns out to be so advantageous, means that there is some type of lag between when the formula is entered and when it is calculated. Parameter values do need to be adjustable, but they do not need to be updated in "real time."

   For instance, the safety stock calculation should change over time, however the benefits of the formula being instantly dynamic have been greatly oversold. My research shows that other factors are far more important than whether safety stocks, or other parameter values for that matter, are instantly updated. There is also the question of whether a safety stock value can be **too dynamic** – that is it responds too quickly to short-term deviations at the expense of the longer-term trend.

3. *Aware Of The Stock Level Of Other Locations*: Optimally, if any parameter value were calculated with an awareness of the stock level at other locations, this would result in higher quality planning output than if each location is treated as an island. It is in fact true that the inventory that is carried at one location is dependent upon the inventory carried at other locations, particularly those locations that are close to the primary location.

4. *Constrained*: It does not make any sense to calculate a safety stock that the company will **not be** willing to carry. In fact, this is one of the major weaknesses of safety stock calculation generally. It is one reason, although there are others, why those that use the standard safety stock calculation often disable the functionality. If the safety stock, or the overall inventory dollars or the physical inventory size, is not constrained in some way, and more stock is planned to be carried than can be carried in reality, and this creates a major problem for stock maintenance.

5. *Values Should Be Calculated from A Global View*: Service level and safety stock, as well as other inventory values, should be calculated, not only in an integrated fashion per product/location combination, but in a way that is consistent with other product locations. Using the same calculations per product location as well as constraining inventory and production consumption so that no single product location or group of product locations receives an over-allocation of supply chain resources accomplish this.

Service Level Calculation Requirements

1. *System Determined Service Levels:* This will probably be a surprise to many; however, as noted in Chapter 5, the biggest need for companies is guidance on what the service levels should be. A calculator, through using any number of assumptions, can determine service levels. This is a very important step in moving the company towards a more rational approach to service level management. This is not to say that the service levels cannot be adjusted manually from this initial setting; however, it does mean that when the service level is adjusted it is clear what the implication is on the other inventory values.

Requirements That Apply to Both Service Level and Safety Stock

1. *Co-calculated with Other Values:* Up to this point, we have been primarily focused on service level and safety stock; however, calculating these values externally to the supply planning application allows for the values to be co-calculated with **other values as well**. This is important

because the more inventory parameters are integrated in terms of their calculation, the less maintenance is involved and the better the overall planning output.

2. *Lead-times:* Neither service level nor safety stock can be calculated without incorporating lead-times. Lead-times determine how much stock must be carried. The longer the lead-time, the more stock must be carried.

3. *High Implement-ability and Maintain-ability*: This is of course not a requirement of the output, but it is a requirement of whatever method or tool is used to set the values. Supply chain departments are typically strapped for resources. This means a high maintenance method or tool is going to have a problem being maintained and has a high potential of falling into disrepair and then disuse. Loosely translated, for Supply Chain departments, the method or tool should meet the other requirements on this list and must be highly implementable and as low-maintenance as possible. This is important because it puts an upper limit on the complexity of the solution.

4. *Low Cost*: Most Supply Chain departments have already spent a good deal of money on systems. They may have hired a large consulting company and paid them a great deal of money. In my experience, the budget for improvement of a system is far smaller than the budget for the implementation of the system. A project which optimizes the parameters of a supply planning system is one of the best values available to an implementing company because it does not require new software but rather simply "tunes" the existing production software.

Other Inventory Parameters

At this point, it is a good time to broaden the discussion to the other inventory parameters that should be co-calculated along with safety stock and service level. The other inventory master data I would like to discuss is the following:

1. *Procurement Min Lot Size:* The minimum procurement lot size. Procurement lot size is often a trade-off between inventory carrying costs and ordering costs.

2. *Production Batch Size:* The minimum production lot size.[2] The production batch size is a trade-off between the costs of production runs, both in the form of changeover costs (cleaning, machine adjustment, etc.) and inventory carrying cost and space considerations.

3. *Reorder Point:* The stock level at which the company should re-order. All supply, and some production planning systems have reorder point planning. All that is required to use this functionality is to identify the product/location combinations that should be placed onto reorder point planning (something that we can do -- although part of a separate forecasting analysis), assign the calculated reorder points and associated parameters.

The final step is to activate reorder point planning as the method that controls the product/location combination in the system. Reorder point planning is a low-maintenance way of managing portions of the product/location database - and frees the planning team to spend more time on other combinations.

The Reality of Supply Planning Parameters
Something that should be understood is that it is a myth that safety stock or service level, or any of these other parameter values above, are set appropriately during an implementation. I have found that in many cases these values are still improperly set years after the implementation is live. The sequence of how supply planning parameters end up being set on new implementations is roughly the following:

1. The system consultants presume that the business team members have the knowledge to set the parameters.

2. The business team members often presume that they will receive assistance from the systems consultants as to the parameters.

---

[2] A company can meet different service levels with either inventory or more flexible manufacturing – that is, they can choose where to incur the costs, and the costs between inventory and manufacturing flexibility are inversely related. Therefore, the application should help them decide what is the correct trade-off between the two costs. Lot sizing applies equally for manufacturing as well as for inventory planning.

3. Time passes on the project while the parameter setting is pushed off to focus on other areas of the implementation.

4. By the time the team circles back to setting parameters it's often too late.

5. Fatigue from both sides, and struggle to meet various project deadlines-often leads to the same parameters values that were in the system to be replaced being ported to the new system. Often there is the token proposal that the parameters can be improved at a later date.

The assumption is often that the original parameters may have been adequate because after all they have been used for some time. My experience with quite a few systems is that in most cases the parameters are greatly sub-optimized.

Secondly, many companies do not establish either sufficient controls over the parameters or periodically review the parameters – for instance to ensure that they meet any of the criteria that have been discussed up to this point.

Thirdly, the sources where companies often think they will receive expert advice on how to set not only these parameters but other system settings tend to come up short. Strategy consultants tend to only be able to describe general principles or to pump up trends like "Lean," but have little follow through to making system improvements.

Systems consultants obviously know their applications well, but do tend to be of the opinions that parameters are a purely business-determined setting, and ask for the values as an input. Therefore, what occurs is that the expertise that is necessary – and this means quantitative expertise – not simply being familiar with the products – is not applied to these values. This is why parameter setting is such a major opportunity at so many companies.

Interestingly, most of the effort by software vendors in this area has been in developing more complex methods. This is done to increase the sell-ability of software, but does not improve the **implement-ability** of the software. In fact in most cases, the more complex the method, the less implementable the software, but the higher potential improvement exists.

The emphasis of consulting companies has by and large been to get new implementations – and ride out the promise of what the future system will be able to do with many billing hours, which means as many consultants as possible being on the project for as long as possible, transferring as little knowledge as possible. The types of improvement projects that are very focused on making fast improvements to existing systems are of little interest to the major consulting companies – there is just not as much money in this type of work as there is in major system upgrades.

Giving the Business the Parameter Support it Needs

On implementations, both software vendors and consulting companies generally have the going in position that these values are all known by the client, and that all that remains is to simply take these values and populate the new system. The reality is that, for the most part, the business sides of companies do not have effective ways of setting these parameters. Just because the parameters pre-exist in an already implemented system **does not mean** they are anywhere close to acceptable values.

The issue is one of specialization. Business resources within companies must manage a system, but are generally not expert at inventory management and parameter setting, and do not have the opportunity to study the topic and apply parameter changes to multiple companies.

Setting the parameters effectively essentially requires a research project where the individual product locations are analyzed, inventory formulations are customized for the specific requirements and needs of the company, and -this point is sorely missed by implementing companies - the parameters are set within the context of the overall product location database so that a usable policy is created.

Planning departments are simply not staffed to perform this type of research. In fact, it is far less cost-effective to try to hire this knowledge in-house because the parameters do not need to be, and in fact should not be, changed - except periodically.

Calculating the Values

All of these values can and should be calculated in an integrated fashion. Companies can expect to see improvements in planning outcomes -less inventory, better service levels - **within one planning cycle** of project completion.

In terms of cost-to-benefit ratio, no software implementation or business consulting improvement project - in the area of inventory management - can compete with this type of parameter calculation project. This is because of the combination of the short duration along with its highly usable and extremely likely improvement in the inventory parameters, which directly results in a better plan.

Finally, out of a supply planning parameter setting project, the company, if it puts the effort in and has the right guidance, can learn what service levels it can afford for different product location combinations. This provides a major benefit not only to Supply Chain but to Sales as well. These service levels could be adjusted by Sales, but the calculated service levels provides a great baseline and understanding of what a profitable service level is for a particular product, and Sales typically appreciates the guidance.

One of the primary problems at many companies is that service levels are not directly tied to the available resources in operations. Sales continually asks for higher service levels, but more resources are often not provided to Supply Chain in order to meet these service level objectives. Supply Chain gets little in the way of value from consulting companies to improve its efficiency.

It's easy to find supply chain consultants who will promote the latest fashion – Lean, Six Sigma, Lean-Six Sigma, inventory optimization, etc. However, the number of consultants who can improve the process and systems as well as understanding solution architecture – as well as customize the solution and approach for the company's needs are few and far between.[3]

---

[3] A serious problem with the rise of the system consulting is that there seems to be less interest in funding business consultants. It is simply assumed by buyers/implementing companies that the systems consultants they bring on board also bring the business knowledge. They think that a consultant who works as an implementation consultant

Supply Chain also often finds that the benefits received by expensive supply planning to be less than advertised – unless they are still trying to get by using the limited supply planning functionality within ERP systems – which are difficult systems in which to perform any type of planning.

Investing time into service level and parameter setting in an intelligent manner is what allows an implementing company to get the quality planning output that was the initial expectation of the supply planning system when purchased. This also creates the critical connection between service levels generally and costs, and differential service levels per product location and costs.

An Inventory Parameter Calculation Project

As soon as one begins talking about external tools to tune production or live systems, many people tend to put up their guard. There is often a great concern that the proponent of using another tool is trying to bring in software to replace the current system. I want to be very clear that the company should not look at this type of project as software that they must purchase.

It also does **not mean** replacing the main supply planning system – rather this process **helps** the currently installed supply planning application by tuning it – by providing it with the input that it requires to provide the best output. For instance, with my calculator that I use for these types of projects,

---

for a particular application understands supply planning from the business perspective – not just within the application.

My observation from evaluating many post-live implementations is that this is not a correct assumption. In order to master the complex supply planning systems most of the consultants I run into tend to have educational backgrounds in computers or engineering – and not supply chain, and many seem to have little affinity for supply chain – they just wanted to work in systems and could have just as easily ended up working in business intelligence or CRM.

For this reason, along with probably several others, the majority of supply planning applications are poorly configured vis-à-vis the actual business requirements. Furthermore, because of limited knowledge transfer – as well as staff turnover and transfer – combined with the constantly increasing complexity of supply planning applications, many companies are running supply planning systems that they either don't entirely understand or very seriously do not understand.

there is nothing to buy because I don't sell it. I simply use it to come up with better parameters.

Important details of these types of projects are the following:

1. *Universally Applicable Output:* The calculator is used to process the records, which your IT group can then upload to the supply planning system. The output works for **any** ERP system and **any** advanced planning system.

2. *No Software to Purchase:* Because there is no software to buy, there is little pushback from IT. An inventory parameter calculation project tunes the existing system with no other investment other than the time to develop the calculator.

3. *Combined Calculation:* Safety stock and service level should be calculated in conjunction with one another. This is completely counter to how things are currently done, but I can prove it is true by showing how values change in conjunction with one another as various inputs change.

4. *Sales and Supply Chain Feedback Loop:* There should be a feedback loop between the service level on the Sales side and the safety stock from the Supply Chain side.

5. *Customization:* Each safety stock/service level improvement project leverages the standard calculator, but adjustments to the calculation can be made depending upon what the implementing company wants to accomplish.

6. *Semi-Permanent or Periodic Review:* Putting this effort and intelligence into setting the service level and the safety stock means that the company has an even greater incentive to reduce manual approximations and override the safety stock values. Once set, the safety stock should **not be** adjusted.

   Because safety stock is such an easy value to change, it is often used as a primary control by not only Supply Chain, but by other groups within the company. While the safety stock should not be changed by planners or used as a lever to control inventory, as time passes the calculations should be updated with more recent information.

This keeps the safety stock values up to date – the normal terminology that describes this is a **periodic review**. This is no different from how the other supply planning/inventory management parameters, such as minimum lot size, are treated. The calculator should be able to co-calculate all of the supply planning/inventory management parameters at the same time, and the parameters should be updated at the same frequency.

The 3S Calculator

After coming to the conclusions that I have explained thus far in this book, I developed the Service Level Scenario Setter and Parameter Optimizer – or 3S for short (see the website for more information on this in terms of the setup and the approach that I use to tune these values. (http://www.scmfocus.com/3S) calculator.)

3S came about after a long road of both finding the common problems with supply planning/inventory management parameters and the limitations I found in performing simulation. 3S rejects the following very common assumptions:

1. *The Business Parameter Setting Assumption:* Parameters can simply be effectively set by the business using their experience with the products.

2. *The Software Vendor Parameter Input Assumption:* Software vendors provide parameter information.

3. *The Independent Assumption:* Parameter information can be effectively set for one product location combination completely independently from the other product locations.

4. *The Centralization of Complexity Assumption:* All of the complexity in supply planning (be it the method or the calculation of stock controls) should be centered within the supply planning application.

Here is a screenshot of the inventory parameter calculator:

3S Service Level Setting & Parameter Optimizer

Output   *
            Export

Selected Service Level	Min	Percent of Demand Over Lead Time	Average Case Demand Per Month	Product Cost	Product Gross Margin	Lead Time (% of Month)	Average Forecast Error (Forecast Lower Than Actual) Over Lead Time	Average (Late) Lead Time Variability	Cost Per Order
0.92	$1	15%	300	$5	$10	100%	10%	7%	$50.00
0.97	$2	25%	500	$5	$7	25%	15%	7%	$50.00
0.91	$5	10%	200	$15	$10	35%	10%	10%	$50.00

This is just a portion of the output side of 3S. 3S requires inputs of things like the maximum number of production changeovers that company is intent on performing in the planning period (which is normally set to a month), the maximum number of pallet spots available in the supply network, the inventory carrying cost, the lost sale multiple (that is how much a company penalizes itself for missing an order or stocking out) – along with a number of other factors.

As you can see from the assumptions that 3S rejects (assumption 4), 3S proposes that complexity can be accounted for outside of the specific supply planning application that the implementing company is using. This allows 3S to tune the parameters and to apply improvement logic **before** the planning system begins its work. This is valuable for two important reasons:

1. Most companies do not use sophisticated supply planning applications (such as SAP SNP, Tools Group SO99 or similar), and still rely upon ERP systems – which use a combination of MRP for the initial supply planning run (this brings material into the supply network and schedules planned production orders), and DRP for the deployment run (which moves material out from the factories and eventually out of the supply network to customers). The major supply planning runs are included in this footnote.[4]

---

[4] S&OP &Rough Cut Capacity Plan: These long range planning threads are generally not

2. Those companies that have implemented more advanced supply planning functionality do not realize that most of these systems do little to optimize parameters. Some advanced supply planning applications have proven to be too much for companies – and this has led to waste. That is money spent implementing systems that have not lead to improved planning outcomes.

3S can either tune a sophisticated supply planning system or can allow even simpler systems – like ERP systems – to plan with far more sophistication assumptions – and without performing a full external planning system implementation. For companies currently using an ERP system that are thinking of moving to a more sophisticated set of supply planning functionality, the first step should be to see if the supply planning parameters can be tuned for the existing ERP system.

This is because this is a far faster way to see improvement in the planning output, and secondly, more advanced supply planning systems use the same supply planning parameters as simpler methods that are employed in ERP systems. In fact, even if a company were to commit to implementing a new and more sophisticated supply planning system, the time to tune the supply planning/inventory management parameters would be ASAP as the existing ERP system needs help immediately, and the new supply planning system may not be operational for many months.

---

part of the live environment. They are used for analytical purposes rather than to drive recommendations to the ERP system.

The Initial Supply Plan (performed by MRP in ERP systems) produces the initial production and procurement plan. It is focused on bringing stock into the supply network, and in creating stock with planned production orders. It can also be called the master production schedule (MPS), if the initial supply plan is run under certain criteria. http://www.scmfocus.com/supplyplanning/2011/10/02/the-four-factors-that-make-up-the-master-production-schedule/

The Deployment Plan (performed by DRP in ERP systems) is focused on pushing stock from locations at the beginning of the supply network to the end of the supply network.

The Redeployment Plan (performed by specialized applications with redeployment functionality or with a custom report). Focused on repositioning stock which is already in the supply network to locations where it has a higher probability of consumption. http://www.scmfocus.com/inventoryoptimizationmultiechelon/2011/10/redeployment/

Secondly, once the new supply planning system is ready to be populated with master data, the parameter information will already have been tuned – therefore investment in parameter setting improves both the current state and the future state.

Simplified Constraints in 3S

The benefits of constraint-based planning have been proselytized for some time. However, implementing constrain based software is much more difficult than generally proposed by software vendors.[5] Interestingly, when companies purchase advanced supply planning applications, they often think they will be able to plan in a constrained manner soon after the implementation. This turns out not to be the case, and few companies have the constraints working properly even years after their constraint-based software is live.

Furthermore, the categories of constraints that buyers/implementing companies actually use are nearly always fewer than what the initially think they will use. While some supply planning systems can be constrained on multiple types of supply planning constraints (production, storage, transportation, etc.) in actual practice it is extremely rare to find supply planning systems **use anything but** production constraints. This is described in more detail in the following article.

http://www.scmfocus.com/supplyplanning/2011/10/02/commonly-used-and-unused-constraints-for-supply-planning/

The benefits of constrained planning are very powerful – as has been explained in many software sales presentations. Without the ability to constrain, planners – or an automated procedure - must move the excess demand to periods of excess capacity in a process called capacity leveling.

---

[5] Constraining is a complex topic, which I am touching on briefly here. For a thorough explanation of constraints, and in particular how to integrated constraints between supply and production planning systems, see the SCM Focus Press book, Constrained Supply and Production Planning in SAP APO. http://www.scmfocus.com/scmfocuspress/select-a-book/constrained-supply-and-production-planning-in-sap-apo/.

If the amount of inventory is in some shape or form constrained (and there are a number of ways of accomplishing this), and if the inventory can be correlated with service level, then the overall level of inventory can be adjusted per product location combination. This can allow the inventory to be allocated in a scientific manner across all of the products, not disproportionally and arbitrarily reduced for some products as it is in most cases. Furthermore, this process should be automated within the calculator.

On the other hand, the safety stock that is carried must be consistent with production constraints as well. Therefore, one can set a maximum number of changeovers in production, so that the resulting safety stock and inventory level does not create more changeovers than production can manage during a period. This means that even planning systems that do not have the ability to constrain (which includes most of the methods that are presently implemented within companies) can be partially constrained or what I call "pseudo constrained," by performing the calculation of inventory values in an external calculator.[6]

Furthermore, constraining in this way is far simpler than constraining within the actual production system. A true constraint-based supply planning application provides a level of constraint sophistication that is far greater than what would be available within a calculator like 3S.

Some supply planning systems have the ability to constrain an individual production line (I won't go into the other supply planning constraint capabilities such as constraining storage because they are so rarely implemented in practice.) However, this is also a great deal more time and effort to setup and to maintain.

---

[6] It is a bit different than what is usually used, and therefore I refer to it as "pseudo" constraints. These pseudo constraints apply to whatever level of aggregation is loaded into the model. This can be the overall product location database or can be a subset of the database for a factory or distribution center or a region. These pseudo constraints interact with how the problem is divided for the model in the following way per type of aggregation.

A major problem is that implementing companies generally do not test if they are capable and can successfully constrain at a higher level before jumping into an application that constrains at the lowest level. Using an external calculator is an excellent way to find out the company's tolerance level for putting the work in to perform constraint-based planning.

S&OP in 3S

A familiar refrain within companies is that things would be much improved if...

> *"We only had an S&OP process that really worked."*

Sales and operations planning or S&OP is a strange animal. First, it brings together individuals from different groups that normally don't coordinate their activities. Second, S&OP processes don't work anything like the textbooks say because the parties (Sales, Finance and Supply Chain/Operations) do not have equal power. Therefore, Sales and Finance tend to tell Supply Chain/Operations what to do – rather than actually asking for their input as an equal partner.

The S&OP process normally relies upon information from the demand, supply, and production planning systems in order to balance supply and demand over the long-term horizon. There are several areas of supply chain planning that seem to have a shortage of software development effort applied to them, and S&OP is one of these areas. There are very few true S&OP software applications, although there are many software vendors that say their applications can do S&OP, and a great number of marketing documents on S&OP that tend to stretch the truth as to how the application actually supports the S&OP process. One of the few vendors to really dedicate themselves to S&OP is Steel Wedge, and while they are presently growing rapidly, the vast majority of S&OP processes don't use any particular S&OP application, but rely upon Excel.

For a number of years, I also followed the conventional view that S&OP should rely upon extracts from the major supply chain planning systems – a design which is also proposed by the major consulting companies. However, after developing 3S – for what was really simply the setting of supply planning parameters, I had the lucky outcome that it was also quite effective at supporting at least part of the S&OP process.

3S naturally shows the relationship between service levels and supply chain constraints, and it can do it very quickly. It is also remarkably dual purpose. When 3S is populated with product and location information to support supply planning parameter adjustment, and has service level values per product location combination, it is immediately ready to be used for S&OP.

Furthermore, it is also a lightweight solution compared to most of the Excel spreadsheets I have seen used in S&OP meetings. I am able to **get to the heart** of the trade off between service levels and operational costs and constraints much more quickly than other approaches I have seen used.

If product price and cost information can also be extracted from the system, the overall plan can also be easily dollarized. Dollarization is necessary in order to tell finance what the costs of providing a level of service will be – however, when more complicated questions arise – such as the costs of adding new production lines, or purchasing more off-site storage, 3S does not provide these answers directly, but rather more external calculation is required to perform the analysis of adding capacity to the system.

Conclusion

Companies buy supply planning functionality in the form of ERP systems, and specialized external supply planning systems or APS systems, thinking that these systems, in great part, hold the answer for improving service levels. This is part of the sales pitch on the part of the software vendor.

The truth is that unless the company purchases an MEIO system, **nothing very much sophisticated** or particularly advantageous for the implementing company is available for either service level setting or safety stock calculation. This approach of relying upon the production system for these values has been thoroughly tested and has repeatedly shown to provide poor outcomes for companies.

I have not sat through all that many sales presentations for supply planning software, however, from observing the knowledge level after these systems have been implemented, it appears very likely that the impression is given that buyers receive calculated values from the system to address parameters. The approach presented in this book is unorthodox and it will not be a message heard by any buyer/implementing company that brings in consulting help from any consulting company that I am aware of.

I have also never seen this approach used at any company I have consulted for. It is original in that I did not copy the concept from any on-site source or book, publication, although it is quite possible that someone else has developed something similar – either a consulting company or someone within an implementing company.

But whoever else has developed something similar, they are not actively promoting it, as I could find nothing like this in my own Internet searches. This is also one of the reasons that the opportunity to improve systems following this approach is so great – it's simply not an area of focus for the entities that would normally be able to make it a focus area.

The unfortunate truth is that buyers/implementing companies are generally not properly informed of the capabilities of the safety stock and service level functionality when they purchase their ERP or APS system. They often work with the settings for years without ever figuring out that there is nothing new in these areas over the system that they replaced.

After years of seeing this issue with my various clients, and reviewing extracted parameters from supply and production planning systems that both made no sense and were poorly maintained, and being asked to find ways to improve the output of supply planning systems, I developed a calculator to tune these settings in a scientific way. This calculator allowed me to adjust the standard dynamic safety stock calculation, which while published in all of the inventory management books, after extensive testing, I found to provide the output that my clients wanted. Therefore, when 3S performs its calculations, a customized safety stock output is generated.

My second conclusion is that most companies need to calculate both service levels and safety stock **outside** of the ERP system or APS system. This can be accomplished with another system, an MEIO system for instance, or it can be accomplished at less expense and less sophistication by the approach described in this chapter.

Whatever approach is used, the tool performing the calculation should account for variability, it should be dynamic, it should be aware of the stock level of other locations, it should be constrained, and it should calculate from the global view of the overall supply network. The approach should also calculate the parameters in a way that is consistent with other important inventory parameters for the same product location combination. This is due to the fact that there is a relationship between all of these parameters (Procurement Min Lot Size, Production Batch Size, etc.).

This is where an external custom application can do something that no other off-the-shelf application that is used or reviewed as the live or production system can do.[7] Rather, these systems tend to treat each of the parameters as independent, allowing them to be set to any value without any coherence across the other parameters.

I never read that this was a poor practice; it became apparent to me that this is a greatly sub-optimal way of setting control data through analyzing the data of many of my clients and experimenting with creating external calculators over a number of years. All of these values can be calculated in an integrated fashion.

Companies can expect to see improvements in planning outcomes - less inventory, better service levels - within a few weeks of project completion. However, to see the full effect of the improvement will require several order cycles as past ordering and scheduling decisions continue to drag on the KPIs. In terms of cost-to-benefit ratio, no software implementation or business consulting im-

---

[7] I have reviewed most of the supply planning systems on the market. Evaluations of various supply planning systems are available at this link. http://www.scmfocus.com/ softwaredecisions/plans/software-selection-packages/

provement project in the area of inventory management can compete with this type of parameter calculation project.

One thing for anyone reading this to realize is that it is an illusion or misrepresentation that safety stock or service level, or these other values above, are set appropriately during an implementation. I have found that in many cases these values are still improperly set years after the implementation are live.

I can walk into almost any company, big or small – and find serious deficiencies in their supply planning parameters. Companies often have a number of excuses – the planners have been busy lately, or a new system was just implemented, or security has been lacking on the system so some people have been making adjustments that they should not have – but the end result is nearly always the same. Therefore, just because the parameters exist in an already implemented system does not mean they are anywhere close to acceptable values.

Conclusion

This book may be surprising to many as it undermines the orthodoxy with respect to service levels and safety stock setting. Most of the modern approaches to managing service levels (such as having Sales provide their best guess as to what service levels should be) as well as managing safety stock (such as using dynamic safety stock calculators in production applications) do not work well enough to continue to use them.

However, the fact that they do not work does not stop these approaches from continuing to be proposed by what are often considered to be the thought leaders in this area – namely the software vendors and the consulting companies. In the vast majority of companies, service level and safety stock management – along with other supply planning/inventory management parameters is in a fairly deplorable state. There is simply very little connecting between Sales and Supply Chain in most companies, with each seeming to being doing their own thing.

Most software, even inventory management or supply planning software, assumes that the service level is known and is simply an input, when in fact companies themselves, while desiring a "high" service level, do not in fact know what it should be - as either an average for their entire product location database or for an individual product or location. Most companies are able to meet their service level targets only "on paper" through the use of various methods that amount to inaccurate accounting for the service levels, and there are a variety of ways to calculate service levels to make them seem higher than they actually are.

Companies can also behave schizophrenically when it comes to the rising and falling **importance** of service level objectives over time. Service levels should be set in a way that is that is considerate of the constraints in the system. These constraints include things like the number of pallet spots available, the available inventory investment, the reliability of the selected suppliers, and the forecast error, among others.

Most companies simply lack the ability to control their service levels and connect the service level to a level of investment or knowledge. Providing a service level of 98% is quite expensive under normal circumstances (the simpler the setup of the supply chain and the fewer products carried, the higher the volume, the easier it is to attain higher service levels – but most companies have difficult and overly complicated supply chains and product location combinations).How do companies know that their customers are willing to actually pay for attaining higher service levels? Service levels are simply arbitrarily set and better tools are needed in terms of setting service levels – as well as connecting the service levels to the operational costs and constraints.

MEIO software is the most advanced supply planning and service level-setting software that currently exists. MEIO is an innovative use of two separate forms of optimization: inventory optimization and multi-echelon optimization. Each answers separate supply chain planning questions.

Inventory optimization answers the question of how much to keep in inventory, while multi-echelon optimization answers the question of where to keep inventory in the supply network.

One of MEIO's major features is the control it gives planners and organizations over service levels. Highlighting their flexibility, MEIO applications can also start from an **inventory goal and work toward the service level**. That is they can work in "forward or reverse." This is very valuable for companies that have a hard cap on inventory dollars that they are willing to allocate.

For those companies that have the interest in spending the time and the money, MEIO has a lot to offer either as the primary or as the secondary system. However, there are also faster and easier ways to get much of what MEIO offers to companies at far less expense and with a higher likelihood of success.

Secondly, following the simpler approach is a great way to get fast improvements even if the company eventually desires to move to a more complete solution. This second way is to create or use an external supply planning/inventory management calculator.

Companies that think that these parameters will be set during the implementation, or that their business users have the answers as to what these values should be will end up being disappointed. Simulation using the production software (in what is referred to as a simulation version) is also not a good away to arrive at these parameter settings as it simply takes too much time and the settings have to be changed individually rather than using a calculator, which calculates all of the values precisely and comprehensively per product location combination.

3S is a calculator I developed, which I use with my clients to tune their system. This approach works because I have tested it with 3S on data from a number of clients. 3S rejects a number of assumptions regarding how supply planning/inventory management parameters are assumed to be managed. These are extremely common assumptions that are made on projects – and it just so happens that none of them are true.

3S can either tune a sophisticated supply planning system or can allow even the simplest of supply planning systems – like ERP systems that rely upon MRP and DRP – to plan with far more sophistication assumptions – and without performing a full external planning system implementation.

Very importantly, 3S allows even a company that does not have software, which can perform constraint-based planning to **access** some constraint functionality through the use of the constraints in the external calculator. This is generally not even known by buyers/implementing companies that think they have to purchase the more advanced systems and engage in a full and complex implementation in order to access constraint based planning functionality.

Finally, another application for which 3S excels at is S&OP. Once 3S is populated with data from the production system, it provides the fastest feedback on service levels versus costs and constraints that I have seen in any tool or software application.

It does not rely upon the planning output of the planning systems, as do most of the S&OP solutions, because it contains its own internal calculation logic. Therefore all that is necessary is to update the product location combinations and their basic data (price, cost, average demand, etc.) along with the constraints (pallet spots, number of changeovers, etc.) and 3S is ready to provide its output.

This takes a significant load off of the production system – which often has a specialized long forecast horizon planning run – that is then extracted and imported into the S&OP "solution," be that an actual application or a series of spreadsheets.

Because this planning run has to calculate for so many periods, it tends to be a scheduled as a weekend job. With 3S, there is the option of simply using the average demand per month per product location combination and simply replicating that for the S&OP planning horizon or using unique demand values. The second approach is much more work.

3S is what I use to accommodate the needs of supply chain parameter setting. However, for the majority of people that read this book, they will never be able to access 3S. Still, the concept of performing supply planning inventory management calculation in an external calculator is an important concept and actually quite vital to the improvement of supply planning systems generally.

What my experience has lead me to conclude is that the conventional approaches to improving supply planning systems do not work very well, and there is very little energy put into evaluating the effectiveness of either the implementation or tuning of supply planning systems.

For supply planning, as well as demand planning and production planning, it is "Groundhog Day" with the same large entities rolling out the same ineffective and threadbare "solutions" all built around unquestioned adherence to principles that never really worked and designed to net the most billing hours for the service providers.

It took me a good deal of time to finally see through the conventional explanations and techniques in this area, and understand that there are far easier ways of doing things than is generally accepted. They won't maximize the consultant's billing hours, but they are effective and fast to implement. A great place to start to make improvements is in the external calculation of supply planning parameters.

References

A Brief History of Just In Time. Strategos Inc.
http://www.strategosinc.com/just_in_time.htm

Bijvank, Marco. Vis, F.A. Iris. Lost Sales Inventory Systems with a Service Level Criterion. European Journal of Operations Research, 2012.

Cohen, M. A., N. Agrawal, and V. Agrawal, "Winning in the Aftermarket." Harvard Business Review (May 2006).

Brynes, Jonathan. What is Wrong With a 95% Service Level.
http://blogs.dcvelocity.com/finance/2011/03/whats-wrong-with-a-95-service-level.html

Byrnes, Jonathan. Islands of Profit in a Sea of Red Ink. Portfolio Hardcover, 2010.

Kieninger, Alex. Westernhagen, Jens. Satzger, Gerhard. The Economics of Service Level Engineering. Hawaii International Conference of System Sciences, 2011

Lee, Calvin. Demand Chain Optimization: Pitfalls and Key Principles. NONSTOP Solutions, 2002.

Lee, Calvin. "Multi-Echelon Inventory Optimization." Evant, 2003.

Lejuene, Miguel A. Probabilistic Modeling of Multi Period Service Levels. European Journal of Operational Research, 2013

Plossel, George. Orlicky's Material Requirement's Planning. Second Edition. Mc-Graw Hill,1984. (first edition 1975)

Plossl, George. Production and Inventory Control: Techniques and Principles. 2nd ed. Prentice Hall, 1985.

Schweitzer, Maurice. Cachon, Gerard P. Decision Bias in the Newsvendor Problem with a Known Demand Distribution: Experimental Evidence

Snapp, Shaun. Constrained Supply and Production Planning in SAP APO. SCM Focus Press. 2013.

Snapp, Shaun. Inventory Optimization and Multi Echelon Planning Software. SCM Focus Press. 2012.

Welsh, Lisa. Stella Service Rates Your Customer Service. Inc., April 2014. http://www.inc.com/magazine/201404/liz-welch/stella-service-rates-your-customer-service.html

Author Profile

Shaun Snapp is the founder and editor of SCM Focus. SCM Focus is one of the largest independent supply chain software analysis and educational sites on the Internet.

After working at several of the largest consulting companies and at i2 Technologies, he became an independent consultant and later started SCM Focus. He maintains a strong interest in comparative software design, and works both in SAP APO as well as with a variety of best-of-breed supply chain planning vendors. His ongoing relationships with these vendors keep him on the cutting edge of emerging technology.

Primary Sources of Information and Writing Topics

Shaun writes about topics with which he has firsthand experience. These topics range from recovering problematic implementations, to system configuration, to socializing complex software and supply chain concepts in the areas of demand planning, supply planning and production planning.

More broadly, he writes on topics supportive of these applications, which include master data parameter management, integration, analytics, simulation and bill of material management systems. He covers management aspects of enterprise software ranging from software policy to handling consulting partners on SAP projects.

Shaun writes from an implementer's perspective and as a result he focuses on how software is actually used in practice rather than its hypothetical or "pure release note capabilities." Unlike many authors in enterprise software who keep their distance from discussing the realities of software implementation, he writes both on the problems as well as the successes of his software use. This gives him a distinctive voice in the field.

Secondary Sources of Information

In addition to project experience, Shaun's interest in academic literature is a secondary source of information for his books and articles. Intrigued with the historical perspective of supply chain software, much of his writing is influenced by his readings and research into how different categories of supply chain software developed, evolved, and finally became broadly used over time.

Covering the Latest Software Developments

Shaun is focused on supply chain software selections and implementation improvement through writing and consulting, bringing companies some of the newest technologies and methods. Some of the software developments that Shaun showcases at SCM Focus and in books at SCM Focus Press have yet to reach widespread adoption.

Education

Shaun has an undergraduate degree in business from the University of Hawaii, a Master of Science in Maritime Management from the Maine Maritime Academy and a Master of Science in Business Logistics from Penn State University. He has taught both logistics and SAP software.

Software Certifications
Shaun has been trained and/or certified in products from i2 Technologies, Servigistics, ToolsGroup and SAP (SD, DP, SNP, SPP, EWM).

Contact
Shaun can be contacted at: shaunsnapp@scmfocus.com

Abbreviations

APS – Advanced Planning and Scheduling
DRP – Distribution Requirements Planning
ERP – Enterprise Resource Planning
JIT – Just in Time
MEIO – Inventory Optimization and Multi Echelon Planning Software
MRP – Material Requirements Planning
PLC – Product Location Combination
3S – Service Level Scenario Setter and Parameter Optimizer
SaaS – Software As a Service
SKU – Stock Keeping Unit
SLA – Service Level Agreement
S&OP – Sales and Operations Planning
TSL – Target Stocking Location

Links Listed in the Book by Chapter

Chapter 1:

http://www.scmfocus.com/writing-rules/

http://www.scmfocus.com

http://www.scmfocus.com/supplyplanning

Chapter 2:

http://www.inc.com/magazine/201404/liz-welch/stella-service-rates-your-customer-service.html

Chapter 6:

http://www.scmfocus.com/supplychaininnovation/2010/10/eric-larkin-andnathan-martin-from-arena-solutions-on-the-benefits-of-saas/

http://www.cisco.com/en/US/products/ps6602/products_ios_protocol_group_home.html

Chapter 7:

http://www.scmfocus.com/sapplanning/2011/10/12/snp-optimizer-sub-problem-division-and-decomposition/

http://www.scmfocus.com/inventoryoptimizationmultiechelon/2010/04/inventory-optimization-definition/

http://www.scmfocus.com/inventoryoptimizationmultiechelon/2007/08/multiechelon-definition/

http://www.scmfocus.com/inventoryoptimizationmultiechelon/2010/01/effective-lead-time-and-multi-echelon/

Chapter 8:

http://www.scmfocus.com/supplychainsimulation/

http://www.scmfocus.com/sapplanning/2009/11/08/scm-simulation-archival-blog/

http://www.scmfocus.com/3S

http://www.scmfocus.com/supplyplanning/2011/10/02/the-four-factors-that-make-up-the-master-production-schedule/

http://www.scmfocus.com/inventoryoptimizationmultiechelon/2011/10/redeployment/

http://www.scmfocus.com/supplyplanning/2011/10/02/commonly-used-and-unused-constraints-for-supply-planning/

http://www.scmfocus.com/scmfocuspress/select-a-book/constrained-supply-and-production-planning-in-sap-apo/

http://www.scmfocus.com/softwaredecisions/plans/software-selection-packages/

Conclusion:

http://www.scmfocus.com/supplyplanning/2014/04/08/safety-stock-calculator/

http://www.scmfocus.com/supplyplanning/2014/04/10/reverse-dynamic-safety-stock-calculation/